IMPLEMENTATION OF THE U.S.-CHINA NUCLEAR COOPERATION AGREEMENT

HEARING

BEFORE THE

COMMITTEE ON INTERNATIONAL RELATIONS HOUSE OF REPRESENTATIVES

ONE HUNDRED FIFTH CONGRESS

SECOND SESSION

FEBRUARY 4, 1998

Printed for the use of the Committee on International Relations

U.S. GOVERNMENT PRINTING OFFICE

50–151 CC WASHINGTON : 1998

For sale by the U.S. Government Printing Office
Superintendent of Documents, Congressional Sales Office, Washington, DC 20402
ISBN 0-16-057332-7

COMMITTEE ON INTERNATIONAL RELATIONS

BENJAMIN A. GILMAN, New York, *Chairman*

WILLIAM GOODLING, Pennsylvania
JAMES A. LEACH, Iowa
HENRY J. HYDE, Illinois
DOUG BEREUTER, Nebraska
CHRISTOPHER SMITH, New Jersey
DAN BURTON, Indiana
ELTON GALLEGLY, California
ILEANA ROS-LEHTINEN, Florida
CASS BALLENGER, North Carolina
DANA ROHRABACHER, California
DONALD A. MANZULLO, Illinois
EDWARD R. ROYCE, California
PETER T. KING, New York
JAY KIM, California
STEVEN J. CHABOT, Ohio
MARSHALL "MARK" SANFORD, South Carolina
MATT SALMON, Arizona
AMO HOUGHTON, New York
TOM CAMPBELL, California
JON FOX, Pennsylvania
JOHN McHUGH, New York
LINDSEY GRAHAM, South Carolina
ROY BLUNT, Missouri
KEVIN BRADY, Texas

LEE HAMILTON, Indiana
SAM GEJDENSON, Connecticut
TOM LANTOS, California
HOWARD BERMAN, California
GARY ACKERMAN, New York
ENI F.H. FALEOMAVAEGA, American Samoa
MATTHEW G. MARTINEZ, California
DONALD M. PAYNE, New Jersey
ROBERT ANDREWS, New Jersey
ROBERT MENENDEZ, New Jersey
SHERROD BROWN, Ohio
CYNTHIA A. McKINNEY, Georgia
ALCEE L. HASTINGS, Florida
PAT DANNER, Missouri
EARL HILLIARD, Alabama
BRAD SHERMAN, California
ROBERT WEXLER, Florida
STEVE ROTHMAN, New Jersey
BOB CLEMENT, Tennessee
BILL LUTHER, Minnesota
JIM DAVIS, Florida

RICHARD J. GARON, *Chief of Staff*
MICHAEL H. VAN DUSEN, *Democratic Chief of Staff*
WALKER ROBERTS, *Senior Professional Staff*
KIMBERLY ROBERTS, *Staff Associate*

CONTENTS

WITNESS

APPENDIX

[1] Classified responses by The Honorable Robert Einhorn can be found in the files of the Committee on International Relations.

IMPLEMENTATION OF THE U.S.-CHINA NUCLEAR COOPERATION AGREEMENT

WEDNESDAY, FEBRUARY 4, 1998

HOUSE OF REPRESENTATIVES,
COMMITTEE ON INTERNATIONAL RELATIONS,
Washington, DC.

The Committee met, pursuant to notice, at 10 a.m. in room 2172, Rayburn House Office Building, Hon. Benjamin A. Gilman (chairman of the Committee) presiding.

Chairman GILMAN. The hearing will come to order.

Our witness today is the Honorable Robert Einhorn, Deputy Assistant Secretary of State for Nonproliferation. Thank you for coming. Welcome.

The central question before us today is how U.S. national interests are served by engaging in nuclear cooperation with China and, in particular, how U.S. nonproliferation objectives are fulfilled by such cooperation.

In a Full Committee hearing on October 11, 1997, the Committee spelled out its criteria for passing judgment on the U.S.-China Nuclear Cooperation Agreement. Included were three basic points.

First, we said the Administration must keep the Congress apprised of its intentions with regard to the agreement. We urged them to brief regularly the Committee and to lay out the Administration's rationale for implementing the agreement before the October 1997 summit. I believe the Administration has worked in good faith to try to fulfill those requests.

Second, we asked that in order to implement the agreement, the Administration must make the required certification and report pursuant to the 1985 and 1990 laws that set conditions on any nuclear cooperation agreement. We said that the certification must stand on its own; that the Administration must adhere to the letter of the law.

The Administration submitted a certification on January 12, 1998. In part, the purpose of today's hearing is to have the Administration make its case for its certification. Until that case is heard, we will reserve judgment on whether the certification meets the requirements of the law.

Third, we said that perhaps—most importantly—the Administration would need to convince our Committee that now is the time to change the status quo with regard to nuclear cooperation with China. In that regard, I reiterate that it is not only China's nuclear nonproliferation record that is on trial. Clearly, Members must be convinced that China has stopped assisting Pakistan's nuclear weapons procurement program and Iran's efforts to develop an indigenous nuclear weapons capability.

Just as importantly, Members need to know that China is engaging in responsible nonproliferation behavior across the board, including all weapons of mass destruction as well as conventional weapons.

In addition, Members need to understand why we have appeared to lower our nonproliferation standards by not insisting that China become a member of the Nuclear Suppliers Group before we engage in nuclear cooperation with them.

Finally, our Members need to be convinced that beyond issuing pieces of paper, China has in place an effective and fully functioning export control system. In that regard, we have been denied the ability to conduct post shipment verifications for our dual use exports into China, a common practice for safeguarding our exports in many countries of the world, including Syria. It should be clear that we have noted the complete absence of any penalties or sanctions in the Chinese export control decrees.

It is in these areas that I do not believe the evidence supports engaging China in nuclear cooperation at this time.

Before proceeding further, there are a couple of procedural matters I want to address. We worked out an arrangement with the Administration whereby we will remain in open session as long as Members have questions to address to Mr. Einhorn that can be answered in our open forum. When it is clear that all questions have been exhausted that can be addressed in an open session, we will continue the hearing in closed session with Mr. Einhorn, to be joined by Mr. John Lauder, who is director of the Nonproliferation Center, Central Intelligence Agency.

The House and Committee rules require that we take a rollcall vote with the majority of the Committee present to go into closed session. Accordingly, I want to alert our witness and the Committee that when we have a majority of the Members present I will entertain a motion to go into closed session. Assuming that vote allows us to go into closed session, we will then continue our session until all Members have exhausted their questions.

At this point I have a series of unanimous consent requests to make. I ask unanimous consent that a copy of the January 12, 1998 certification package submitted by the President be inserted in the record at the appropriate place, without objection.

[The information referred to appears in the appendix.]

Chairman GILMAN. I ask unanimous consent that the background memorandum prepared by the Congressional Research Service be placed at the appropriate place in the record.

I want to commend Shirley Kan at the CRS for her work in support of our Committee on that issue.

[The information referred to appears in the appendix.]

Chairman GILMAN. Further, I ask unanimous consent that a document entitled "China's Nonproliferation Words vs. China's Nuclear Proliferation Deeds" be inserted in the record at the appropriate place.

[The information referred to appears in the appendix.]

Chairman GILMAN. If there is no objection, we will consider those as having been adopted.

Mr. Hamilton, would you care to make an opening statement?

Mr. HAMILTON. Thank you very much, Mr. Chairman. I want to join you in welcoming our distinguished witnesses, Robert Einhorn, Deputy Assistant Secretary of State for Nonproliferation, and Mr. John Lauder, Director of the Nonproliferation Center of the CIA, and to extend my thanks to them for coming.

I want to thank you also, Mr. Chairman, for scheduling this very important hearing on the U.S.-China agreement on peaceful uses of nuclear energy.

I think it is important to say quite clearly at the outset that China's overall nonproliferation record leaves much to be desired. Even in the nuclear field, for instance, China has apparently assisted Pakistan's unsafeguarded nuclear program and engaged in significant nuclear cooperation with Iran. It exercises little supervision over its exports of nuclear materials, equipment or components.

Until now, no President has been able to make the required certifications regarding China's nonproliferation policies, without which peaceful nuclear cooperation between our countries is prohibited by law.

At the same time, it is important to recognize that China has taken steps in recent years to join most of the rest of the world in the effort to halt the spread of weapons of mass destruction. It has acceded to the Nonproliferation Treaty, the cornerstone of the nonproliferation regime; signed the Chemical Weapons Convention; promised to abide by the guidelines and parameters of the Missile Technology Control Regime designed to halt the spread of ballistic missiles; has stopped nuclear testing; and has signed the Comprehensive Test Ban Treaty. It has worked with us and our international partners to contain the threat posed by North Korea's nuclear ambitions. It has pledged not to assist in an unsafeguarded nuclear facility anywhere in the world.

Now, some of my colleagues have argued that the President should not certify China in the nuclear area because we are not satisfied with China's record in the areas of missiles and chemical weapons. Indeed, I think in your testimony here in a few minutes you will tell us that the Administration recognizes the progress of the Chinese in the nonnuclear areas as lagging behind the progress on nuclear issues. I think there is no question that Chinese behavior in nonnuclear areas is not satisfactory. More progress is required, and the Administration must continue to press China very hard.

The question now is what is the best way to ensure that China's record on nonproliferation continues to improve. First, we are obviously going to have to continue to monitor Chinese nonproliferation behavior very closely.

Second, we have to remember that we do not give up our leverage now that the President has made the certification we will be examining today. We can deny export licenses for goods and technology at any point if China reverts to unacceptable behavior. We will, in other words, continue to have a stick alongside the carrot of peaceful nuclear cooperation.

Finally, I think it is important not to allow the perfect to become the enemy of the good. At some point we have to pocket the progress we have achieved, rather than hold out for additional concessions and risk that the Chinese will conclude negotiations with us at some point.

Last, there are risks with proceeding with peaceful nuclear cooperation with China, but we should also knowledge that there are risks as well in not proceeding.

In any event, these are important hearings and I am very pleased our witnesses are with us and that you, Mr. Chairman, have scheduled it. Our judgment, of course, will be based on the evidence of the law and an overall assessment of whether this agreement promotes the American national interest.

Thank you, Mr. Chairman.

Chairman GILMAN. Thank you, Mr. Hamilton.

Do any other Members seek recognition?

Mr. Bereuter.

Mr. BEREUTER. Thank you, Mr. Chairman. I want to say at the beginning of the hearing that the Administration has a significant burden to prove that all the requisite certifications under U.S. law are met, and that this Member will, as I'm sure my colleagues intend, carefully scrutinize the certification made by the President of the United States to the Congress.

Nevertheless, the Congress should not rush to move the goal posts on this process. It is always easy for us to second-guess and say that the Administration could have negotiated one more concession from China on any set of negotiations. It was true with the intellectual property rights negotiations, true with the WTO negotiations, and it could be true with the nuclear talks.

However, we must remind ourselves of several key points. First, written guarantees from the PRC to control the export of nuclear technology to countries such as Iran and Pakistan is a major nonproliferation achievement. It will give us a bright line benchmark to gauge the PRC's willingness to honor its commitments in the future.

Second, it is in the U.S. interest to ensure that China has a safe nuclear power generation program.

Third, it is in our interest to ensure that China not overly rely on dirty coal for their energy needs.

Fourth, it is in our interests to ensure that China not look to Iran for its energy needs.

Fifth and finally, it is in our interests to help build reactors that will be built with or without us. It is clear that since the United States has imposed an export embargo on nuclear technology to China, that China has turned to the Canadians, the Russians, the French and others to begin building what will amount to be an important part of the energy infrastructure for the 21st century. I intend to keep these things in mind and urge my colleagues to do likewise.

Thank you, Mr. Chairman.

Chairman GILMAN. Thank you, Mr. Bereuter.

Mr. Menendez.

Mr. MENENDEZ. Thank you, Mr. Chairman. I want to thank you for holding this hearing. I have some very serious and very real concerns about China's commitment to the nuclear cooperation agreement. Among the outstanding concerns are China's continued sales to Pakistan of missile-related technology and materials, China's sale to Iran of nuclear technology and equipment, and its assistance to Iran in developing medium-range ballistic missiles at the missile industrial complex near Tehran.

Recently there were more than 100 Chinese and North Korean experts working on this site, and that is both a cause for concern and skepticism. In November I sent a letter to the President, and several other Members did, asking that he certify that China has halted all exports of nuclear technology to nations with unsafeguarded nuclear facilities before implementing the 1985 agreement.

Presidents Reagan and Bush were unable to provide the necessary certification, and I hope, Mr. Secretary, that you will be able to shed some light on what progress China has made that allowed President Clinton to sign the required certification on January 12 of this year. In particular, I am concerned about reports that China has sold ring magnets and a high temperature furnace to Pakistan for use at a nuclear reactor being built in Pakistan without any IAEA safeguards in 1996.

We also know that China continues to be a key supplier to Iranian nuclear projects. China has built a system for enriching uranium to be used at the safeguarded site in Karach in Iran, and speculation continues about China's plans to sell a facility to Iran to convert uranium ore into uranium hexafluoride gas which could be enriched to weapons-grade material.

Given these outstanding reports, we need to seriously consider the possibility that the Chinese are making nice in public while simultaneously undermining the agreement and the security of the Middle East and the subcontinent. So I hope, Mr. Secretary, you will speak to some of these issues and what steps the United States is prepared to take if the Chinese continue to sidestep the agreement.

Thank you, Mr. Chairman.

Chairman GILMAN. Thank you, Mr. Menendez.

Mr. Fox.

Mr. FOX. Thank you, Mr. Chairman. I join my colleagues in thanking you for your leadership in holding these hearings, along with Mr. Hamilton, and I thank Mr. Einhorn and Director Lauder for joining us today.

As we move through this hearing I think it is important that we have as one of our hopeful goals that the Administration explain why it is in our national interest to engage in nuclear cooperation with China, and in particular how our U.S. nonproliferation objectives will be forwarded by this cooperation with regard to certification. Has China ended its longstanding practice of assisting Pakistan, and why would the United States extend their cooperation to a country which is not a member of the Nuclear Suppliers Group?

We only have to look to the fact of China's nonproliferation words versus their deeds. In 1997 they stated, "I wish to emphasize once again China has never transferred nuclear weapons or relevant technology to other countries, including Iran." Then the actual reports of facts show that China is a key supplier of nuclear technology to Iran and supporting over $60 million annually. Yet in 1996 China's position was clear, it does not advocate or encourage nuclear proliferation. Yet another report shows China was the single most important supplier of equipment and technology for weapons of mass destruction worldwide.

I hope we can get to the bottom of this and move ahead jointly with the Administration. I thank the Chairman for holding these hearings.

Chairman GILMAN. Thank you, Mr. Fox.

Is there any other Member seeking recognition?

If there are no other Members seeking recognition, we again welcome Robert Einhorn, Deputy Assistant Secretary for Nonproliferation, Bureau of Politico-Military Affairs in the Department of State, responsible for nuclear, chemical, and biological missile nonproliferation and regional arms control.

Mr. Einhorn previously served as senior adviser to the policy and planning staff, Department of State, responsible primarily, again, for arms control and nonproliferation, and was formerly the representative of the U.S. Arms Control and Disarmament Agency at the START negotiations.

Welcome, Mr. Einhorn. You may submit your full statement or you may summarize it, whichever you deem appropriate.

STATEMENT OF ROBERT EINHORN, DEPUTY ASSISTANT SECRETARY FOR NONPROLIFERATION, BUREAU OF POLITICO-MILITARY AFFAIRS, DEPARTMENT OF STATE

Mr. EINHORN. Mr. Chairman, thank you very much for giving me the opportunity to appear before the Committee. I would like to have permission to submit my prepared statement for the record and then open with some briefer remarks.

Chairman GILMAN. Without objection.

Mr. EINHORN. Thank you, Mr. Chairman.

The United States has a major national security interest in China being a force for stability in the 21st century, committed to a variety of critical international norms, including nonproliferation. But, as a number of Members have already pointed out this morning, China's past record on proliferation has been a source of serious concern.

In the 1980's it provided assistance to Pakistan's nuclear weapons program. It has not shown sufficient restraint in transfers of missile equipment and technology, dual use chemicals and chemical production equipment, and conventional arms, especially to Iran and Pakistan. It has not had effective export controls, so that even when China has wanted to show restraint, its ability to show restraint has sometimes been inadequate.

Given these problems, the Administration has assigned a very high priority to encouraging a positive evolution in China's policies and practices in the area of nonproliferation. We saw a promising opportunity to do so in negotiations on implementing the long-dormant 1985 U.S.-China agreement for nuclear cooperation.

The Chinese have wanted to implement this agreement in order to enable them to buy U.S. nuclear equipment and technology which they apparently believe could make an important contribution to their ambitious nuclear energy plans. But the agreement had been approved by the Congress on the condition that it could not be implemented until the President certified, in effect, that

China was not assisting any nonnuclear weapons state to acquire nuclear weapons.

In early 1985 we entered into negotiations on steps that China could take in the area of nuclear nonproliferation to meet U.S. legal requirements for implementing the 1985 agreement. In the course of over 2½ years we believe we have achieved some important results.

First, China committed in May, 1996 not to provide assistance to unsafeguarded nuclear facilities in Pakistan or anywhere else. Since then, we are not aware of any transfers of equipment or material by Chinese entities to Pakistan's unsafeguarded program. We have discussed with Chinese officials some cases of potential concern involving contacts between Chinese entities and elements associated with Pakistan's nuclear weapons program. However, our current information indicates that China appears to be acting consistently with its 1996 pledge.

Second, China has agreed to phase out its nuclear cooperation with Iran, even cooperation under IAEA safeguards. It has already suspended the sale of two nuclear power reactors, canceled the transfer of a uranium conversion facility, and turned down Iranian requests for other sensitive equipment and technology. And it has provided a clear assurance that it is not going to engage in new nuclear cooperation with Iran, and that it will complete a few existing projects within a relatively short period.

Third, China is putting in place for the first time a comprehensive nationwide system of controls over nuclear-related exports. These controls are embodied in formal directives and regulations issued by China's State Council, and they involve control lists substantively identical to those used by the Nuclear Suppliers Group.

Fourth, last October China became a member of the Zangger NPT Exporters Committee, the first time China has joined a multilateral nonproliferation export control regime.

These recent steps satisfy and in some instances even exceed the standards set by U.S. law for implementing the 1985 agreement. The progress can be measured in concrete steps already taken, not just promises for future behavior.

Moreover, these specific steps should be viewed together with other actions China has taken during the 1990's that demonstrate its growing acceptance of international nonproliferation norms. Mr. Hamilton mentioned a number of those steps: China's adherence to the nonproliferation treaty, its termination of nuclear testing and its signature of the Comprehensive Test Ban Treaty, as well as its support for a Fissile Material Cutoff Treaty.

Taken together, these developments constitute a marked positive shift in China's nuclear nonproliferation policies and practices. On the basis of this record, the President announced this past October 29 that he would submit to the Congress the certifications and reports required to implement the 1985 agreement.

Mr. Chairman, the implementation of the 1985 agreement will bring important benefits to the United States. It will provide an effective means of encouraging China to live up to its recent commitments in the area of nuclear nonproliferation.

It is essential to point out that the agreement makes China eligible to receive U.S. nuclear exports. It does not guarantee that

China will receive them. Under our nuclear licensing procedures, individual transactions will have to be approved on a case-by-case basis. If the Chinese do not abide by their assurances, we can withhold approval of any new licenses and we can even revoke previously approved ones.

We will be monitoring China's behavior very carefully. If and when problems or uncertainties arise, we will raise them promptly with the Chinese. With the 1985 agreement in effect, and prospects for continued nuclear cooperation potentially at risk, the Chinese will have strong incentives to prevent or stop any activities inconsistent with their commitments.

Activating this agreement will also give us the most promising basis for making further progress in the nonproliferation area. The Chinese have already agreed that, with implementation of this agreement as a necessary first step, we can soon begin government-to-government cooperation in such important areas as nuclear materials security, international safeguards, and nuclear safety.

We also plan in the period ahead to press the Chinese for progress on missile, chemical, and conventional arms issues. These are issues where serious problems remain in China's policies and practices. Implementing the nuclear cooperation agreement will show the Chinese that if they make hard decisions and bring their behavior into conformance with international norms, then they can expect that there will be benefits for both sides. This will encourage the Chinese to take similarly hard decisions on nonnuclear issues.

While proliferation has been the main focus of our efforts to promote implementation of the agreement, we have also been aware of the likely commercial benefits. Activation of the agreement will allow U.S. companies to participate in the fastest growing nuclear power market in the world today.

These benefits are difficult to quantify, they are difficult to predict. But the market in China for nuclear reactors alone is a multibillion dollar one, so we would expect the benefits in terms of the U.S. balance of trade and industrial job creation at home to be substantial.

Mr. Chairman, the Administration believes the arguments for our proceeding now with implementation of the agreement are strong. At the same time, we listened carefully to concerns raised by you and by some other Committee Members in November's floor debate. I would like to turn briefly to three of those concerns.

First, some Members asked whether the Chinese could be trusted to live up to their new commitments in light of the past record. We would respond that the issue before us is not that of the historical record, which we recognize is unsatisfactory. It is whether China is now abiding by its commitments and will do so in the future.

Chinese behavior for close to 2 years now has been encouraging. It appears to reflect a level of seriousness and commitment we simply did not see before. Will this positive pattern continue? Will Beijing be up to the challenge of applying its new export control system to China's numerous and far-flung governmental and private entities? The reality is that we cannot pretend to know the answers to these questions.

We must, therefore, approach implementation of the agreement with a healthy skepticism. President Reagan's advice to trust but verify is clearly warranted here. So we will be monitoring China's behavior carefully, and the Chinese will know that any actions inconsistent with their commitments will jeopardize future cooperation.

Second, some Members suggest that implementation of the agreement be made conditional upon improvement in China's export policies and practices, not just in the nuclear area but in the missile, chemical, and conventional arms areas as well.

The Administration can report, in this connection, that some significant progress has already been made in the nonnuclear areas, including China's commitment no longer to export complete MTCR-class ground-to-ground missiles, its adherence to the Chemical Weapons Convention, and its recent pledge to stop transfers to Iran of antiship cruise missiles and related production technology.

But we would be the first to say that progress in these nonnuclear areas has lagged behind progress in the nuclear issues. A major focus with China in the months ahead will be to press for additional progress in the nonnuclear agenda.

However, we could not support linking implementation of this nuclear agreement to movement on these nonnuclear issues. Our laws are very clear on this. They say that implementation requires performance only in terms of China's nuclear nonproliferation policies and practices. To insist now on additional steps would be seen as moving the goal posts and would stand very little chance of success.

Third, a number of Members suggest that we further postpone implementation of the agreement to acquire a better track record for evaluating Chinese behavior. Our response is that in a very real sense we already have a substantial track record. We focused heavily on China's nuclear export activities in recent years, and especially since May, 1996.

As noted earlier, the recent record is promising. Uncertainties remain. We fully appreciate that. But such uncertainties will almost surely continue to arise. It is in the nature of intelligence-gathering and in the kinds of activities we are focusing on.

The best way to resolve these uncertainties is not to postpone implementation. Rather, it is to proceed now with implementation and to use the incentives provided by the agreement—namely, China's stake in nuclear cooperation with the United States—to press for answers to our questions and insist on strict compliance.

Moreover, China is moving ahead now with its future nuclear power plans. If we wait much longer, China will opt for non-American partners. We could lose not just the commercial benefits but the important nonproliferation benefits already achieved.

Chairman GILMAN. Mr. Einhorn, if I might interrupt you, we are trying to hold a quorum here to go into our closed session. Let me interrupt you for a moment so that we can do some housekeeping.

As the Chair mentioned earlier, we would like to take testimony from Mr. Lauder following the testimony of Mr. Einhorn. Mr. Lauder, as you know, is from our Central Intelligence Agency, and he cannot testify in open session. Members will also have the opportunity to hear further from Mr. Einhorn if they would like him to elaborate on some matters he has raised earlier.

Because disclosure of classified national security information would endanger the national security, we would like to proceed later today in closed session. Since a quorum appears to be present, I will recognize the gentleman from Nebraska, Mr. Bereuter, to make a motion at this time.

Mr. BEREUTER. Mr. Chairman, I move pursuant to rule 4(b) of the rules of the Committee that at a time and date to be subsequently designated by the chairman or his designee, after consultation with the Ranking Democrat Member, the Committee shall receive testimony in closed session on the grounds that disclosure of the testimony, evidence, or other material to be considered would endanger the national security.

Chairman GILMAN. Is there any debate on this question?

The question, then, is on the motion of the gentleman from Nebraska. Under the Rules, the vote must be taken by rollcall. The majority of the Committee must be present.

The Clerk will call the roll.

The CLERK. Mr. Gilman?

Chairman GILMAN. Aye.

The CLERK. Mr. Gilman votes yes.

Mr. Goodling?

[No response.]

The CLERK. Mr. Leach?

[No response.]

The CLERK. Mr. Hyde?

Mr. HYDE. Aye.

The CLERK. Mr. Hyde votes yes.

Mr. Bereuter?

Mr. BEREUTER. Aye.

The CLERK. Mr. Bereuter votes yes.

Mr. Smith?

[No response.]

The CLERK. Mr. Burton?

[No response.]

The CLERK. Mr. Gallegly?

[No response.]

The CLERK. Ms. Ros-Lehtinen?

[No response.]

The CLERK. Mr. Ballenger?

[No response.]

The CLERK. Mr. Rohrabacher?

Mr. ROHRABACHER. Aye.

The CLERK. Mr. Rohrabacher votes yes.

Mr. Manzullo?

[No response.]

The CLERK. Mr. Royce?

[No response.]

The CLERK. Mr. King?

[No response.]

The CLERK. Mr. Kim?

Mr. KIM. Aye.

The CLERK. Mr. Kim votes yes.

Mr. Chabot?
Mr. CHABOT. Aye.
The CLERK. Mr. Chabot votes yes.
Mr. Sanford?
Mr. SANFORD. Aye.
The CLERK. Mr. Sanford votes yes.
Mr. Salmon?
[No response.]
The CLERK. Mr. Houghton?
Mr. HOUGHTON. Yes.
The CLERK. Mr. Houghton votes yes.
Mr. Campbell?
Mr. CAMPBELL. Yes.
The CLERK. Mr. Campbell votes yes.
Mr. Fox?
Mr. FOX. Yes.
The CLERK. Mr. Fox votes yes.
Mr. McHugh?
Mr. MCHUGH. Yes.
The CLERK. Mr. McHugh votes yes.
Mr. Graham?
[No response.]
The CLERK. Mr. Blunt?
[No response.]
The CLERK. Mr. Brady?
Mr. BRADY. Yes.
The CLERK. Mr. Brady votes yes.
Mr. Hamilton?
Mr. HAMILTON. Aye.
The CLERK. Mr. Hamilton votes yes.
Mr. Gejdenson?
Mr. GEJDENSON. Yes.
The CLERK. Mr. Gejdenson votes yes.
Mr. Lantos?
[No response.]
The CLERK. Mr. Berman?
Mr. BERMAN. Yes.
The CLERK. Mr. Berman votes yes.
Mr. Ackerman?
Mr. ACKERMAN. Yes.
The CLERK. Mr. Ackerman votes yes.
Mr. Faleomavaega?
[No response.]
The CLERK. Mr. Martinez?
[No response.]
The CLERK. Mr. Payne?
[No response.]
The CLERK. Mr. Andrews?
[No response.]
The CLERK. Mr. Menendez?
[No response.]
The CLERK. Mr. Brown?
[No response.]
The CLERK. Ms. McKinney?

[No response.]
The CLERK. Mr. Hastings?
Mr. HASTINGS. Yes.
The CLERK. Mr. Hastings votes yes.
Ms. Danner?
Ms. DANNER. Aye.
The CLERK. Ms. Danner votes yes.
Mr. Hilliard?
[No response.]
The CLERK. Mr. Sherman?
Mr. SHERMAN. Aye.
The CLERK. Mr. Sherman votes yes.
Mr. Wexler?
Mr. WEXLER. Yes.
The CLERK. Mr. Wexler votes yes.
Mr. Rothman?
Mr. ROTHMAN. Aye.
The CLERK. Mr. Rothman votes yes.
Mr. Clement?
Mr. CLEMENT. Aye.
The CLERK. Mr. Clement votes yes.
Mr. Luther?
[No response.]
The CLERK. Mr. Davis?
Mr. DAVIS. Yes.
The CLERK. Mr. Davis votes yes.
Chairman GILMAN. The Clerk will call the absentees.
The CLERK. Mr. Goodling?
[No response.]
The CLERK. Mr. Leach?
[No response.]
The CLERK. Mr. Smith?
[No response.]
The CLERK. Mr. Burton?
[No response.]
The CLERK. Mr. Gallegly?
[No response.]
The CLERK. Ms. Ros-Lehtinen?
[No response.]
The CLERK. Mr. Ballenger?
[No response.]
The CLERK. Mr. Manzullo?
[No response.]
The CLERK. Mr. Royce?
[No response.]
The CLERK. Mr. King?
[No response.]
The CLERK. Mr. Salmon?
[No response.]
The CLERK. Mr. Graham?
[No response.]
The CLERK. Mr. Blunt?
[No response.]
The CLERK. Mr. Lantos?

[No response.]

The CLERK. Mr. Faleomavaega?

[No response.]

The CLERK. Mr. Martinez?

[No response.]

The CLERK. Mr. Payne?

[No response.]

The CLERK. Mr. Andrews?

[No response.]

The CLERK. Mr. Menendez?

Mr. MENENDEZ. Aye.

The CLERK. Mr. Menendez votes yes.

Mr. Brown?

[No response.]

The CLERK. Ms. McKinney?

[No response.]

The CLERK. Mr. Hilliard?

[No response.]

The CLERK. Mr. Luther?

[No response.]

Chairman GILMAN. The Clerk will report the vote.

The CLERK. On this vote there were 24 "ayes" and zero "noes".

Chairman GILMAN. The motion is agreed to. I thank the Members for responding to the quorum call.

Mr. Einhorn, please continue.

Mr. EINHORN. Thank you, Mr. Chairman. I only have a few concluding remarks.

Mr. Chairman, Members of this Committee attach great importance to China's adherence to international nonproliferation norms. So does the Administration.

The record of recent years demonstrates clearly that the most promising means of promoting progress with the Chinese now is through tough, frank, persistent engagement, using a combination of carrots and sticks. Implementing the 1985 agreement now, in full conformity with U.S. law, will provide an essential vehicle for pursuing this effort.

We know this is a hard issue for you and for Members of the Committee. The Administration recognized it was a hard issue nearly 3 years ago, but promoting changes in China's behavior in the proliferation area was seen as critical to U.S. national security, so we decided to take it on.

We put a major effort into this, and at all levels. We believe we have made some real progress. Any open-minded observer can see that. But the job is incomplete and the outcome is uncertain. We know that. We are committed to press ahead to demand strict compliance with existing commitments, and to push for progress where progress has so far been inadequate.

But to continue making progress and finish the job, we must remain engaged. We cannot insist on near-term perfection and walk away if it is not achieved. We have to be in this for the long haul, however frustrating it may sometimes be. But we need the tools, and the most important tool at this juncture is implementation of the 1985 agreement. We urge your support. Thank you, Mr. Chairman.

[The prepared statement of Mr. Einhorn appears in the appendix.]

Chairman GILMAN. Thank you, Mr. Einhorn.

Mr. Einhorn, as you know, China continues to provide assistance to safeguarded facilities in Pakistan. The second paragraph on page 7 of the unclassified report included in the certification states, "We have not asked that China end safeguarded nuclear cooperation with Pakistan as a condition for implementing the peaceful nuclear cooperation agreement."

I ask, why not, Mr. Einhorn? And let me continue a moment.

The next sentence in that paragraph reads, and I quote, "But we have on numerous occasions warned China that the risk of providing assistance to the peaceful nuclear program of a country such as Pakistan is that some of the assistance may be diverted to unsafeguarded activities."

Mr. Einhorn, I am asking you, does China clearly understand that nuclear cooperation will be halted, and by that I mean that NRC licenses will not be granted, if there is conclusive evidence that Pakistan diverts Chinese assistance from its safeguarded to unsafeguarded program?

Mr. EINHORN. Thank you, Mr. Chairman. We did have a long discussion with the Chinese about acceptance of full-scope safeguards as a condition of nuclear supply. We urged China to join members of the Nuclear Suppliers Group and insist on full-scope safeguards.

But the Chinese pointed out to us that the Chinese are now engaged in supply of a power reactor to Pakistan under safeguards, and insistence on this principle, full-scope safeguards, would have disrupted their ongoing nuclear cooperation arrangement under safeguards with Pakistan. They were not ready to do that. We did impress that upon them.

We didn't insist on it at this stage for a number of reasons. Foremost, acceptance of full-scope safeguards as a condition of supply is not a requirement of the NPT. It is not a requirement for nuclear certification under the current laws, so we did not press. We did secure China's agreement to join the Zangger Committee, the NPT Exporters Committee, which doesn't require full-scope safeguards as a condition of supply.

This was a very important step, and it brings China into multilateral discussions for the first time. We will continue to press the Chinese to go the additional step beyond the NPT to accept full-scope safeguards as a condition of supply.

At the same time, we have had discussions with the Chinese about the difficulties of engaging in safeguarded cooperation with a country like Pakistan that also has unsafeguarded facilities. We have warned them of the risks, and we have suggested to them that they take strong steps to ensure that their safeguarded assistance not be diverted to unsafeguarded facilities or uses. If we were to discover that their safeguarded assistance were being diverted to such unsafeguarded uses, we would want to take it up with the Chinese and talk to them about what strict measures they could adopt to avoid any such diversion.

Chairman GILMAN. Is that the extent of our remedy, that we would talk to them about that? What are the red lines? As the Administration's top expert on nonproliferation, could you explain to our Committee what kinds of Chinese behavior would lead you to recommend that nuclear cooperation be halted?

Mr. EINHORN. If the Chinese acted inconsistently with the assurance they have given to us, if they would provide assistance to unsafeguarded facilities anywhere in the world, this would be a violation of our commitments and this would be grounds for withholding our consent to nuclear licenses.

On the question of a third country diverting China's safeguarded assistance to an unsafeguarded facility, this is something that we would want to raise with China, and to talk to them about adopting additional measures to avoid such diversion.

We would also want to speak to the IAEA and urge them to take strong steps to prevent such a diversion because, after all, they have the responsibility to apply safeguards to that material and to ensure that it is not diverted.

Chairman GILMAN. Mr. Einhorn, let me explore just a little further.

If the Chinese heavy water is determined to be in Khushab, are you prepared to recommend that our Nation halt nuclear cooperation with China? Has China been specifically advised that nuclear cooperation would be halted under those circumstances?

Mr. EINHORN. I think the question of this Khushab reactor is one that can best be taken up in closed session. You are raising a hypothetical case as to whether there is Chinese heavy water there or not. There is a question of whether there is Chinese heavy water there or some other heavy water, and how it got there.

These are all complicated questions, and it is perhaps easier to discuss these various possibilities in closed session.

Chairman GILMAN. Mr. Einhorn, I am not asking you for evidentiary conclusions. I am asking you, if there were to be found heavy water there, what would be our policy?

Mr. EINHORN. Again, it is hard to answer that in the abstract. If there were to be heavy water there, the issue is, where did they get the heavy water? Did they produce it themselves? Did they get it from another country, not China, or produce it themselves? Was it diverted by Pakistan from a safeguarded facility?

Chairman GILMAN. Assume it came from China. Would that be a violation?

Mr. EINHORN. If China provided heavy water outside of safeguards to the Khushab facility, that would be a violation.

Chairman GILMAN. What would our recommendation be then?

Mr. EINHORN. Our recommendation would be the same if it occurred after May 1996 as in the case of any provision of assistance to an unsafeguarded facility anywhere in the world. We would say this would be a violation of China's assurances to us, and this would be grounds for withholding cooperation with them.

Chairman GILMAN. My time has run out.

Mr. Hamilton.

Mr. HAMILTON. Mr. Einhorn, I just want to get the procedure in mind here. The President has made the certification under the law. There is a 30-day period. And what is that, continuous legislative days? So it will end up when, approximately?

Mr. EINHORN. It is 30 days of continuous legislative session, and so depending on the kind of weekends you spend here, it could end up as soon as, I think, March 7 or so. And if you take a few 4-day weekends over the next month or so, it could go until perhaps late April.

Mr. HAMILTON. And the agreement goes into effect unless the Congress passes a resolution of disapproval, is that correct?

Mr. EINHORN. That is correct, sir.

Mr. HAMILTON. And that of course is subject to a veto, so what you really are confronted with here, if you want to cancel this agreement, is that you have to deal with that Presidential veto and get two-thirds of the vote, right?

Mr. EINHORN. That is correct, sir.

Mr. HAMILTON. So in all likelihood, then, the agreement goes into effect in that time period.

Now just in a very broad way, with all of this difficulty we have in the U.S.-China relationship, why is it in the U.S. national interest to go ahead with this U.S.-China Nuclear Cooperation Agreement? In the broadest terms, why is it in our interests?

Mr. EINHORN. Because encouraging China to conform to nonproliferation norms is in our vital security interests, and we believe that is the best way of continuing to press the Chinese to go forward, as you put it in your opening remarks, to pocket the gains we have already achieved and to move on. We think this provides useful leverage to keep moving the Chinese in the right direction.

Mr. HAMILTON. Now, the people that have been critical of this agreement on several scores most often mention that we ought to attain more progress on other nonproliferation issues like missiles and chemical weapons, the so-called nonnuclear issues, before we move forward with this agreement. You spoke to this in your testimony but I want to make sure we can nail it down.

As I understand it, you said that U.S. law today is very clear on that point, and that in order to implement the 1985 agreement we require performance in terms of Chinese nuclear nonproliferation policies. That is in the law. Congress passed that and the President signed it. Was that law enacted in 1985?

Mr. EINHORN. 1985, and in addition we had the 1990 law.

Mr. HAMILTON. So we ourselves have set the standards to judge here in law?

Mr. EINHORN. That is correct. The standards are very clear. The reports we were to make, the certifications that we were to make, apply to the nuclear record.

Mr. HAMILTON. If we come along and say to China, ask them to perform with respect to nonnuclear standards in both missiles and chemical weapons and all the rest of it, then we ourselves are, in effect, changing the rules of the game, moving the goal posts, are we not?

Mr. EINHORN. That would be correct. Let us remember, we have asked the Chinese to do some very difficult things here. We have asked them to curtail certain cooperation with Pakistan. We have asked them to stop even safeguarded cooperation with Iran. These are hard steps for any sovereign government to take, but they took them on the expectation that we would meet our end of the bargain. If we would move the goal posts now, what incentives would the Chinese have to take additional hard steps in the area of chemical and missile and conventional arms?

Mr. HAMILTON. You recognize that in those areas progress has been less than we would like to see?

Mr. EINHORN. There has been progress, and I enumerated some examples, but certainly it has been less than we would want.

Mr. HAMILTON. If you look back over several years here of Chinese performance, and I think it is always important to get a trend rather than a snapshot, are you more impressed with the progress that has been made by China in meeting the international norms on nonproliferation, or are you more impressed with China's flouting of those norms?

Mr. EINHORN. In the 1990's, and given the steps that I mentioned in my statement, we see a marked positive shift in China's behavior. Is it perfect? No, of course not, we need to see further movement. But the trend, as you put it, the pattern is absolutely clear. I think it is clear to the greatest skeptic on this point. Our view is that we have to continue this trend, and implementing this agreement is the best way to continue it.

Mr. HAMILTON. Thank you, Mr. Chairman.

Chairman GILMAN. Thank you, Mr. Hamilton.

Mr. Rohrabacher.

Mr. ROHRABACHER. Thank you very much. Would you characterize the Chinese as having basically an honest relationship with us or a dishonest relationship with us?

Mr. EINHORN. I would characterize it as a self-interested relationship with us. I think they do what is in their own national self-interest. We have to understand those interests, try to find a way that our interest is served by their choosing to move in the direction of their own interest. Implementing this nuclear cooperation agreement I think is win-win for both of us.

Mr. ROHRABACHER. Let me ask it in a different way, then, if you don't want to answer the question that I asked. Would you say that they basically have a truthful relationship with us or an untruthful relationship with us?

Mr. EINHORN. Again, if you are getting at some of the historical record, I don't want to be in a position to certify the veracity of some previous Chinese statements. That would be a tough burden on me or anyone else. The issue is current behavior, and we need to measure current behavior. That is the standard.

Mr. ROHRABACHER. So the current behavior is what you have to focus on? In order for us to move forward with trying to assume that they are OK today, we just have to block out the past?

Mr. EINHORN. We have to be conscious of the past, and in being conscious of the past we need to see the kind of pattern we have been discussing. It has been improvement.

Mr. ROHRABACHER. Let me ask you about the past, then, besides blocking it out and just ignoring it.

In the past when the Chinese were involved with violating these nonproliferation requirements, would they simply thumb their nose at the requirements and say, "We are not going to abide by this," or did they lie to us about it?

Mr. EINHORN. Again, rather than talk about this Chinese statement or that Chinese statement, I would choose to look at their behavior. As I said in my opening statement——

Mr. ROHRABACHER. You refuse to look at their behavior?

Mr. EINHORN. Absolutely not. We need to look at their behavior.

Mr. ROHRABACHER. I am asking about their behavior in the past. There was a certain behavior.

Mr. EINHORN. I understand.

Mr. ROHRABACHER. Did they say, "We don't care about your requirements," or did they say, "We are obeying these requirements," and just lie about it? Which one was it?

Mr. EINHORN. Let me refer you to my prepared statement. In it we point out that in the 1980's China engaged in actions—namely, support for Pakistan's unsafeguarded nuclear program—that would have been violations of the NPT had China been a party to the NPT at that time. That was egregious behavior. We recognize that openly.

The point is, has that behavior changed? We believe that there has been a change.

Mr. ROHRABACHER. So you are suggesting that if there is some word that is given on their part, that we can trust their word now. Is that what you are saying?

Mr. EINHORN. I am not saying that we should rely on trust. As I mentioned before——

Mr. ROHRABACHER. Verify.

Mr. EINHORN. Given the past, we have to apply a healthy skepticism. We have to use our monitoring capabilities to find out whether they are living up to their word. If they are not, we can suspend further cooperation.

Mr. ROHRABACHER. To your knowledge, are they being truthful with us today?

Mr. EINHORN. As I mentioned before, the signs in recent years are encouraging.

Mr. ROHRABACHER. That is not what I asked you.

Mr. EINHORN. No, I am going to answer it.

For example, the very important pledge they made in May, 1996, not to provide assistance to unsafeguarded nuclear facilities, we don't have any evidence that China has indeed transferred material or equipment to Pakistan's unsafeguarded nuclear program.

Do we have questions? Are we sure about the future? Of course we have questions.

Mr. ROHRABACHER. Let me be more specific. Rather than getting this run-around answer, let me be more specific with you. Do you know of a case through your sources of intelligence information in which the Chinese at this moment, in the area of nonproliferation, are lying to us?

Mr. EINHORN. Congressman, I would encourage you to remain here for the closed session and we can get into specifics.

Mr. ROHRABACHER. You can bet I am going to do that.

Mr. EINHORN. But what we are focusing on this morning is the record in the area of nuclear nonproliferation, where we can say we are seeing real positive signs. In some of the areas the record is disappointing.

Chairman GILMAN. The gentleman's time has expired.

Mr. Berman.

Mr. BERMAN. Thank you, Mr. Chairman.

Mr. Einhorn, first I just want to tell you that I don't know of anybody in the U.S. Government who works harder to try to achieve what I think are the critical goals of reducing proliferation of weapons of mass destruction than you do. So I just want to thank you for what you do for us. It sounds like a song or something.

A couple of questions. Why do we have a different standard for nuclear cooperation with Iran—that is, end all nuclear cooperation with Iran, safeguarded or unsafeguarded—than we do with Pakistan? And I hope you will not draw an implication from that question that I think we should curtail our approach toward nuclear cooperation with Iran.

Mr. EINHORN. First, Congressman Berman, thank you very much for those kind remarks.

On the question of Iran and Pakistan, right now fortunately we believe Iran's nuclear weapons program is at an early stage. We believe that any nuclear cooperation with Iran, even under safeguards, could make a contribution to Iran's nuclear weapons aspirations. Even if not directly, it could provide the expertise, the infrastructure. It could move Iran up the nuclear learning curve, so we would discourage any nuclear cooperation with Iran, even under safeguards.

Pakistan is in a different situation. It has a much more mature nuclear program, and especially it has a much more mature nuclear weapons program. We do not believe that continued safeguarded cooperation, if effectively safeguarded, would contribute to Pakistan's nuclear weapons program.

Would we prefer that there be no nuclear cooperation with states without full-scope IAEA safeguards? Yes, we would. But we have to take it a step at a time, and the most important step for China to take was to terminate all unsafeguarded cooperation with Pakistan.

Mr. BERMAN. In your answer to Chairman Gilman you spoke of the Chinese resistance to any nuclear cooperation under safeguarded conditions because of a nuclear reactor project that they are constructing for Pakistan. Is it your sense that it is that specific project that pushes the Chinese position, that this is sort of almost a contract sanctity kind of an issue? They want to finish that project, and at that particular point China would take another look at the question of ending nuclear cooperation with Pakistan?

Mr. EINHORN. I think the Chinese believed that having already taken certain steps to limit or cut off cooperation with Pakistan, they could not take the additional step of disrupting peaceful nuclear cooperation continued under safeguards.

Perhaps sometime in the future when some time has passed, and especially if no new plans for nuclear cooperation exist between China and Pakistan beyond this one 300-megawatt reactor, China will come to the conclusion that it can afford to insist on full-scope safeguards and essentially stop cooperating with Pakistan altogether. But I think doing it now would be seen as an abrupt shift that the Chinese would have felt could have done real damage to their political relationship with Pakistan.

Mr. BERMAN. The President states I guess in his certification that China's nuclear cooperation with Iran has significantly lessened. What does that mean? Is China still assisting in the Iranian nuclear program?

Mr. EINHORN. China was Iran's main supplier of nuclear equipment and technology under safeguards. It was the main provider. What we have seen is a gradual curtailment, and now we have a commitment, a clear assurance from China, that it will phase out all nuclear cooperation.

We had the cancellation of this uranium conversion facility. Mr. Menendez mentioned it earlier. This was a very serious problem. It was a key link in the chain of Iran's nuclear weapons program. They canceled it. They suspended the sale of two nuclear power reactors. They turned down Iranian requests for some other sensitive cooperation.

Now they have pledged to us, no new cooperation, and completion of a few existing projects within a relatively short period. One of those projects is already over. So we are getting to the point where there is very little going on between China and Iran.

Mr. BERMAN. Mr. Chairman, I would ask, have we verified that the June 1997 list of controlled nuclear items that the Chinese have claimed is identical to the Nuclear Suppliers Group trigger list is in fact identical, that their export control list is what it is claimed to be and supposed to be?

Mr. EINHORN. We have two lists. One list we got in September. We have looked at it carefully. It is substantively identical to the nuclear trigger list.

The list we got in June is a dual-use list. We are proceeding methodically through the translation of it. It appears to be substantively identical to the NSG's part 2 dual-use list. A final list on dual-use items will come out by mid–1998, and we will make sure that this is substantively identical to the NSG lists. But we have no reason to believe that they are not identical.

Chairman GILMAN. The gentleman's time has expired.

Mr. Brady.

Mr. BRADY. Thank you, Mr. Chairman. Mr. Einhorn, thank you for being here today and your testimony.

Like other Members, I am skeptical about this agreement. I am skeptical because in issues of human rights, religious persecution, protection of intellectual property rights and open markets, the Administration counsels Congress to be patient; that this historical, ancient Chinese ship of state is slow to change, and that this engagement will work.

But on the issue of nuclear assistance to rogue nations, where their track record is very poor, we are given the impression that this ship of state can essentially turn on a dime and can change in a very short period, which seems very inconsistent with their track record and the Administration's position in so many other areas dealing with China.

So my question is, I think you are right to read the trends, and that is fair. I think it is absolutely consistent for us to, in any contractual agreement, to discuss performance and the measurement of performance and our reaction if they don't perform.

My question is, more specifically, can you share with us how we will measure their performance, and not just that an export control system is in place, but the outcome of it? How many of the measurement indicators are objective and independent, and don't measure a symptom but in fact the true actions that are going on underneath it, that are at the heart of this, that will determine our ability and the Administration's ability to ensure that this agreement is being lived up to?

Mr. EINHORN. Mr. Brady, you are absolutely right. We need to see real deeds, not just words, not just commitments. It is important that China has put in place these regulations and directives and published their control list, but the true test will be implementation of this new system.

So far, in the last couple of years we monitored behavior carefully and we have a number of indicators. One indicator is, are we getting reports of continued shipments of material or equipment to Pakistan's unsafeguarded program? The answer is no, we haven't gotten those reports, which is an encouraging indicator. We saw some cooperation with Iran going forward, plans for pursuing the sale of power reactors. Those were suspended. We saw plans for constructing the sensitive uranium conversion facility. That was canceled. We know that.

So we see indicators, but look, the returns are not all in. There are inherently going to be uncertainties in this. We will see, in our intelligence, ambiguities that will take a while to sort out. When we get into closed session, Mr. Lauder could explain some of the complexities, but there are objective indicators. We are not relying just on paper commitments.

Mr. BRADY. Could you, just because I am new around here and still learning the process, could you share with our office and the Committee a list, in the future or fairly soon, about some of those indicators specifically, so we can become more knowledgeable about it?

Mr. EINHORN. We can do that on a classified basis, and I mention to you something that your Committee staff knows very well. We are available to come to brief Members, to brief staff, to keep you currently informed on developments in these areas. We would like to do that.

Mr. BRADY. Thank you.

Mr. Chairman.

Chairman GILMAN. Thank you. Mr. Menendez.

Mr. MENENDEZ. Thank you, Mr. Chairman. Thank you for your testimony and for your service, Mr. Secretary.

Let me ask you, in response to one of my colleague's questions and in your testimony here, with reference to China easing away from Iran, participation with Iran, the wording here is important, because they say China has suspended the sale of two nuclear power reactors to Iran and canceled the uranium conversion facility. We are happy to see that cancellation. It is a major issue of great concern. Now, why suspend the sale of the nuclear power reactors and not cancel the sale?

Mr. EINHORN. Mr. Menendez, I don't know. It may be a polite way of telling the Iranians it is a cancellation. I think maybe that is the case.

Mr. MENENDEZ. Is it any less polite to cancel the uranium and not cancel—maybe it is the lawyer in me, but when you suspend something, you leave open the possibility that it can be reengaged. When you cancel something, you cancel it, have to start a whole new negotiation. Why not a cancellation of the nuclear power reactors to Iran?

Mr. EINHORN. Well, I guess the way the Chinese see it, there is not much proliferation risk in power reactor transfers. But we explained to them we saw a risk in it, and beyond that, they had some siting problems and financial difficulties with the sale of the power reactors. Given all of these considerations, they basically agreed to take it off the table, and I think that is how they would regard it today.

I don't mean to suggest that there is any real difference between the two. I think the practical reality is that the Chinese are not moving forward with the power reactors or with the transfer of this uranium conversion facility, and they gave us a clear assurance that they would not engage in nuclear cooperation.

Mr. MENENDEZ. Is there any reason why we would not seek a cancellation of the nuclear power reactors?

Mr. EINHORN. I think we saw a clear assurance that China would not engage in cooperation with Iran other than two specific projects that they enumerated to us, and those two specific projects did not include the power reactors. So I think we have gotten a very explicit assurance that they are not going to pursue the power reactor sale.

Mr. MENENDEZ. Let me ask you, with reference to another statement in your record, in the statement on page 2 you said that an acute deficiency in China's nonproliferation record has been the absence of an effective nationwide system of controls for sensitive exports, and even when it has been willing to exercise restraint, its ability to do so has been particularly limited with respect to dual-use goods and technologies.

Why has that changed? Is that not still existent?

Mr. EINHORN. They have taken, in the last few years, steps to improve that. You cited, sir, in your opening remarks the case of the ring magnets. Here is a case where some dual use items, fairly simple equipment, ring magnets, were transferred to an unsafeguarded facility in Pakistan for Pakistan's uranium enrichment program. We think that one of the reasons for this was that China had an inadequate basis of control over these dual-use items. We think they have taken steps since then to correct this.

The ring magnet case was a real embarrassment to China, because what it indicated was that either China was intentionally helping Pakistan's program, or it didn't have the ability to control its own system well enough to prevent this assistance from going to Pakistan. This caused them, as I mentioned, real embarrassment internationally, and I think there was——

Mr. MENENDEZ. Do they have the ability now to control it? Are we satisfied they have that ability now?

Mr. EINHORN. They have put in place since then real changes in their structure, in their laws, in their legal authority. It appears to be doing some good. But again, it takes a while to put in place a fully effective system, and the returns are not in.

Mr. MENENDEZ. One last question. Going back to the suspension of the nuclear reactors to Iran, what if they reengaged, lifting the suspension, and went ahead and made an agreement? Even though

I know you are going to tell me you don't foresee it, what if they did? Would that be a violation in terms of our understanding?

Mr. EINHORN. Would be inconsistent with our understanding.

Mr. MENENDEZ. That would have us do what?

Mr. EINHORN. We have made clear to the Chinese that our willingness to proceed with nuclear cooperation depends on their living up to their commitments.

Mr. MENENDEZ. So we would halt the nuclear cooperation?

Chairman GILMAN. The gentleman's time has expired. The Committee will stand in recess and will reconvene following the vote.

[Recess.]

Mr. ROHRABACHER. [Presiding.] The Committee will come to order. I am going to be chairing here until the Chairman returns. Mr. Gilman has asked me to perform his duty for a few minutes.

Mr. Einhorn, could you give me a little bit of an understanding of what kind of money we are talking about in putting new restrictions on the Communist Chinese Government? What kind of money would they be deriving, or how much money did they derive in the past from these exchanges of nuclear technology? How much do we think they are denying themselves with our putting restrictions on them, or by agreeing to these restrictions, I should say?

Mr. EINHORN. Mr. Rohrabacher, it is very hard to predict the economic implications of implementing the 1985 agreement, because the amount of reactor sales that U.S. firms could enjoy will depend entirely on commercial arrangements between U.S. firms and the Chinese Government.

I should point out, though, that China has a nuclear power program, a nuclear power plant. It plans to have a certain amount of electricity generated by nuclear power by the year 2010, 2020, and so forth. Now, they will meet those requirements either through purchasing American reactors or French or Russian or Canadian.

So when you say how much do we deny, or how much money do we give, it is not a question of our giving because they are going to spend that hard currency to buy reactors. The question is where are they going to spend it.

Mr. ROHRABACHER. That is actually not the direction I was going in. How much money are they making from Iran? What I am saying, Iran and Pakistan, and many other countries we are talking about here that are the recipients of Chinese technology, how much money is being given to them by these countries?

Mr. EINHORN. I see what you are getting at.

Mr. ROHRABACHER. That we are asking them to forego that.

Mr. EINHORN. I understand that. I think with Iran, the main big ticket item was the two power reactors. The Chinese are obviously foregoing a significant amount from Iran from foregoing those two power reactors. A lot of the other cooperation was not very high in dollar equipment value, so I think basically the Chinese made a calculation, do we want to cooperate with Iran or do we want to cooperate with the United States. The Administration, and the President personally, basically put that choice to the Chinese: With whom do you want to cooperate? And the Chinese made the decision, and they wanted to cooperate with the United States, and not necessarily for any dollar reasons. I think they had broad reasons for doing that.

Mr. ROHRABACHER. Were the Chinese then losing $1 billion with the Iranians for these contracts?

Mr. EINHORN. I don't know what the contracts were or the negotiations were. But for two power reactors, it could well have been more than $1 billion.

Mr. ROHRABACHER. OK. In terms of the possibility that the Chinese are still engaged with selling nuclear technology to the Iranians or Pakistanis, you are telling us today that is a thing of the past and that they agreed not to do that?

Is part of your testimony that if this is still going on, it is being done by rogue companies and not as a policy of the government?

Mr. EINHORN. Let me be clear. On Iran, the agreement is to phase out all nuclear cooperation. Our estimate is that they are only engaged in cooperation in one remaining project.

For Pakistan, the commitment is to terminate all unsafeguarded cooperation. They have not agreed to terminate their support for a nuclear power reactor at Chasma in Pakistan, so that will continue presumably toward completion.

Mr. ROHRABACHER. OK. I will go on to my colleagues in one moment.

Then you are saying that the activities that are going on in this direction with Iran, they are being carried out—you are saying that they are over with? I am giving you a chance now to say that they are over with officially, but there might be some things going on below the surface or nonofficially.

Mr. EINHORN. What the Chinese have done is said that they are going to phase out the cooperation. There is still some low-level cooperation taking place. Within a few years that should be terminated.

Mr. ROHRABACHER. If the Chinese resume their cooperation with the Iranians and we find evidence of that, what will be your policy or the policy of the government?

Mr. EINHORN. This then gets to the question where I was saved by the buzzer. It was Congressman Menendez's question. I will give you my own view, and obviously I can't speak for the Administration on that.

If China were to go ahead and sell power reactors to Iran, I would consider that inconsistent with China's commitment to us not to engage in new nuclear cooperation with Iran. I would recommend under those circumstances that we withhold our approval of nuclear cooperation with China.

Mr. ROHRABACHER. I understand you are stating that as your position. I would hope that this Administration will state very clearly for the Chinese exactly what they can expect if they follow that policy; rather than having it your opinion, that it should be delineated. They should know what price they are going to pay if they go down that path or continue to go down that path, and we should also demand an honest exchange when we are talking with these people.

Frankly, in the past it doesn't sound like they have been truthful to us, and we should demand truth and we should give them the truth of our policies, this is what will happen to you if you go that other direction.

Mr. EINHORN. I would agree with you, Congressman. Let me just say one thing. We did say to the Chinese when we concluded this arrangement on Iran that our willingness to go forward with implementation of the 1985 agreement did depend on their meeting their commitments with respect to Iran. So we did state that at an authoritative level.

Mr. ROHRABACHER. Earlier on in our relationship with the Chinese there were the words "strategic ambiguity" used. And it is not just this Administration, but I am afraid that the United States has been afraid to just lay it on the line, to let these people know exactly what their actions will bring about. I am not just saying it is this Administration, it has been true for quite a long time. That doesn't do either one of our countries any good.

Mr. Sherman.

Mr. SHERMAN. Thank you, Mr. Chairman. I think a lot of what I have to say builds on what you have had to say. The Chinese are focused on their own economics. I don't think giving nuclear weapons to Iran is in their long-term interest. I could see a day when the Iranians support secessionist movements in the western provinces of China, which are predominantly Muslim.

But the Chinese are rather clever and they are focused on the bottom line. They get some money from Iran and Pakistan, and they may get a better deal with oil by cooperating on Iran as well. They get some limited economic benefit from this nuclear cooperation. They don't get anything they couldn't buy from Europe. They may get a better value, they may get a better price. Every public works purchaser that I'm aware of in the United States would like to have another competent bidder involved in the job.

But this nuclear cooperation status gives China only limited and modest economic benefit. The big economic benefit that China gets is the $55-billion-a-year trade surplus with the United States that they receive because they have most-favored-nation status.

I think the most important goal is to contain the spread of weapons of mass destruction, and our most important goal with China is to make sure that they are full partners in that effort. Yet, our tools for achieving that, unfortunately, are rather limited. If we don't give them nuclear cooperation, they buy the nuclear reactors from another country.

What they have chosen to do in response to this very, very modest carrot is they comply a little bit, they refuse a little bit, and they lie a little bit. And if they get caught, then maybe they will just have to buy the French nuclear reactors. Big deal.

What we need is another tool. Most-favored-nation status is unfortunately the nuclear bomb of changing economic relations. What we need is, instead, a smart bomb. I would hope this year when we look at MFN, it is not just an all-or-nothing vote; no MFN status, the business community goes crazy, the votes are there to extend it, we are told the United States will enter into a depression, et cetera, et cetera, et cetera.

Instead, we ought to have an opportunity to deny China 10 or 20 percent of the benefits of MFN; determine what the tariff structure would be if they were denied MFN, look at the tariff on each class of goods if they were given MFN, deny 10 or 20 percent of that benefit. With that kind of weapon, with the ability to raise tariffs by a few percentage points and cut their exports to the United States by $5, $10 or $15 billion, I think we would get the kind of responsiveness that we need: full cooperation, not hesitant, partial cooperation on the surface, with a little lying included in some of that.

With that in mind, I do have a question for the witness. It is somewhat similar to the previous questions you have addressed. That is, can you simply tell us, does China continue to provide ballistic missiles and ballistic missile technology to Iran?

Mr. EINHORN. Ballistic missiles, no. Ballistic missile technology, yes.

Mr. SHERMAN. And chemical weapons?

Mr. EINHORN. Chemical weapons, no. And to our knowledge they have never provided chemical weapons to anyone. Dual-use chemical precursors, dual-use chemical production and equipment technology, yes. We see continuing cooperation there.

Mr. SHERMAN. Are there precursors that China will sell to Iran that our allies in Europe would refuse to sell? I mean, all technologies and chemistry used in the creation of chemical weapons.

Mr. EINHORN. All our allies in Europe are members of the Australia Group, and they are very conscientious about meeting their requirements. The Australia Group has a long list of chemical precursors, and our allies exercise great caution in selling anything on that list to Iran.

The problem with China is that it has joined the Chemical Weapons Convention (CWC), which is a good thing, but the controls required by the CWC are narrower than those required of the Australia Group, so you have precursors controlled by the Australia Group and not controlled by the CWC. We need to encourage the Chinese to adopt a stronger international standard.

Mr. SHERMAN. Mr. Chairman, if I could just make a comment, we are not going to see honest and full cooperation from China on all of our efforts until we simply say, not that we might not export something to China, but until we threaten their import stream to the United States.

Mr. ROHRABACHER. Thank you, Mr. Sherman. I would hope that you would be supporting our efforts on the floor to make sure that no money from Export-Import Bank or the World Bank would be provided, or guarantees for loans for business in China, which is somewhere between most-favored-nation status and——

Mr. SHERMAN. My focus is on limiting, threatening, or conditioning Chinese exports to the United States. I tend to like U.S. exports to China.

Mr. ROHRABACHER. Even if they are setting up manufacturing companies and putting people out of work?

Mr. SHERMAN. Again, the focus is on jobs for Americans, and the way to achieve that is to increase exports and to condition imports.

Mr. ROHRABACHER. Thank you.

Mr. Berman, do you have further questions?

Mr. BERMAN. No.

Mr. ROHRABACHER. On the last question, I didn't quite understand the answer that you gave to Brad, the last answer. Could you say that a different way so I could understand it in terms of these chemicals that are being sold by China to Iran?

Mr. EINHORN. The problem with the chemical trade is that you can sell a lot of chemicals and equipment that have dual uses. They can be used for legitimate civilian purposes. They can also be used in a chemical weapons program. Nobody really says "DX nerve agent," but if you are not careful, you can sell ingredients that could enable a recipient to make nerve agents, and so forth.

Mr. ROHRABACHER. I see.

Mr. EINHORN. Virtually everything we are concerned about is of this dual-use nature.

Mr. ROHRABACHER. What you are suggesting, then, is Iran or China may be unintentionally selling these types of chemicals to Iran that would permit them to produce chemical weapons, unintentionally?

Mr. EINHORN. I don't believe China as a government wants Iran to have chemical weapons. China has a decentralized and very extensive chemical industry, and in the past we have seen Chinese companies sell chemical ingredients, chemical precursors, to Iranian entities that we believe are actually part of Iran's chemical weapons program. And in fact in May, 1997, less than a year ago, we imposed trade sanctions on seven Chinese entities for making this contribution to Iran's chemical program.

What we need to do with the Chinese Government now is to get them to tighten up their system so that all Chinese entities behave more responsibly, and that they get government approval for the kinds of transfers that contribute to the chemical weapons program in Iran.

Mr. ROHRABACHER. I will have to say that every time I talk, and it is not just this Administration and it is not just you, but it seems that we are always bending over backwards to give the very best analysis that we can possibly give to these bums. I mean, these people, what do they have to do to prove their intentions? I mean, when they sell nuclear technology to somebody, they mean us ill if that person or that country they are selling to happens to be an enemy to the United States.

And it just it seems to me, whether it is the answer you just gave or answers we have heard not just from you but from the Administration, we are always trying to give them the benefit of the doubt. I don't know, when do we reach the threshold of saying they have lied to us so often in the past that we are no longer going to give these people the benefit of the doubt?

Mr. EINHORN. Congressman, we didn't give them the benefit of the doubt when we imposed sanctions against Chinese entities for helping Iran's chemical weapons program.

Mr. ROHRABACHER. I think that you are giving the benefit of the doubt to the leaders of China, saying that they don't have an iron-fisted control over what happens in their country. It is one thing to explain away rogue companies and rogue elements down there in Tsinkiang or someplace, but in fact we are talking about a very powerful central government that has it in their ability to carry out an order that they give from Beijing.

Mr. EINHORN. Congressman, you are raising a very, very important question, maybe the most fundamental question in dealing with China on this. I would suggest when we go into closed session you ask Mr. Lauder about these points.

The reality is that especially in the case of dual-use equipment and technology, and certainly in the chemical industry, there is a lot of decentralization, and especially when you are dealing with chemicals that could be used for pesticides as well as for nerve agents, you are not getting high-level central control. The Chinese have to adopt a stricter approach toward the control. But it is very possible, and we believe that the senior-most Chinese officials are not aware of this.

Mr. ROHRABACHER. I will ask these two questions that Mr. Gilman wants, to make sure we get them on the record.

One last thing, what about Libya?

We haven't mentioned the Chinese relationship with Libya. Are they involved with these same types of questionable dealings with the Government of Libya?

Mr. EINHORN. Libya has been under a very substantial U.N. embargo for quite some time, and dealings with Libya are very minimal. In terms of contacts with some of the Libyan programs, I suggest we defer this to the closed session.

Mr. ROHRABACHER. OK. Fine. Thank you.

Chairman GILMAN. [Presiding.] Thank you, Mr. Rohrabacher, for sitting in for us while we were voting.

Mr. Einhorn, just one or two questions and then we will go into closed session. In your testimony you argue that we can best modify China's nonproliferation policies and practices by supporting implementation of the 1985 agreement. You also argue that if the Chinese engage in bad behavior, that then we will halt further cooperation with China.

Why should this Committee have any confidence that our Nation will halt nuclear cooperation with China, given the Administration's difficulties in imposing sanctions pursuant to nonproliferation sanction laws? And isn't such an argument particularly implausible, given the tremendous commercial pressures that you would be under in recommending a halt to cooperation?

Mr. EINHORN. I do not think it is implausible, Mr. Chairman. A moment ago I cited an instance in May, 1997 when we imposed trade sanctions against Chinese chemical companies for assisting Iran's chemical weapons program.

Also, as you know, we have imposed trade sanctions against China twice for transfers of M–11 related items to Pakistan. But the case that is most germane to our subject here is the nuclear one, and I cited it in my prepared statement.

When we had the ring magnet problem, if you remember, the Administration used authority at its disposal actually to put a hold on all Export-Import Bank loans to China in early 1996. This was not just loans to the Chinese entity that had engaged in the questionable transaction, it was a hold on all Export-Import Bank loans to China for that 3-month period. I am sure that this registered on the Chinese. They understood what was involved in this. I think this demonstrated our seriousness in dealing with the problem.

Chairman GILMAN. Thank you.

One more question, Mr. Einhorn. It is my view that our Nation should hold China to a higher standard of goals than the ones the Administration set for "sufficient progress" toward ending nuclear proliferation.

One important goal in nuclear nonproliferation policy of all major nuclear suppliers, except China, is a requirement for full-scope safeguards that were intended to prevent diversions to other nuclear facilities. Although our Nation has championed full-scope safeguards and all 35 members of the Nuclear Suppliers Group require them, the President has certified China, despite China's failure to adhere to this international norm.

You argue that it was not an achievable goal to have China require full-scope safeguards before Presidential certification. So I am wondering if the Administration was driven by the need to have goals that are attainable or deliverable by the time of the U.S.-China summit in October 1997, which precluded the difficult negotiation NSG membership would entail.

Is it not a drop in U.S. nuclear nonproliferation standards to ease off the pressure on China to require full-scope safeguards? And further, is proceeding with the agreement a pardon for China as it continues to flout the international norms as the sole nuclear supplier to Pakistan, a nation that has refused to sign a nuclear nonproliferation treaty and refuses to allow inspections at all facilities?

I know that is a mouthful, but if you could address those, I would welcome it.

Mr. EINHORN. Mr. Chairman, you asked if we were driven by the deadline of the October 29 summit in essentially setting standards for compliance. We were driven by the requirements of our law. We think the nuclear certification package meets all of the requirements of our law.

One of those requirements is not to insist that China adopt a policy insisting on full-scope safeguards as a condition of supply. This clearly goes beyond our certification requirements. It even goes beyond the requirements of the NPT. That is clear because the Nuclear Suppliers Group didn't adopt that position until 1992, when the NPT came into force in 1970. So full-scope safeguards goes beyond our legal requirements and the NPT requirements.

We want China to require full-scope safeguards. In Pakistan, hopefully, when we keep pressing on this, ultimately they will agree with us and join the consensus of all nuclear suppliers.

Chairman GILMAN. We hope that will come about. The Administration has yet to demonstrate to Congress it has put in place procedures and mechanisms designed to address criticisms of the General Accounting Office in 1994 with regard to the study of licensing procedures for dual-use nuclear exports.

In its study, GAO found inadequate criteria for selecting pre-license checks and post-shipment verifications, ineffective methods used to perform these inspections, and the lack of verification of government-to-government assurances against nuclear end uses.

Can you tell us why China still insists that no post-shipment verifications can be undertaken by our government officials to check on the end use of our dual-use exports to China?

Mr. EINHORN. It is interesting you raised this question, Mr. Chairman, because this goes to a very important provision of our agreement for cooperation with China. What this agreement includes is an arrangement for visits and exchanges of information that enables us to verify firsthand that China is living up to its commitments and not diverting anything we supply to uses not provided for in the agreement.

But we have a memorandum of understanding. It lays out procedures. It gives us the right, after shipment—you mentioned post-shipment verification. We have the right on a regular basis to visit any reactors we sell, to visit any components, any materials we provide, and to assure ourselves firsthand that these materials and equipment have not been diverted to nonpeaceful uses. This is very clear. We have submitted this to the Congress. It is there in black and white for you to see.

Chairman GILMAN. Thank you.

Mr. Rohrabacher, any further questions of Mr. Einhorn before we proceed to a closed session?

Mr. ROHRABACHER. No.

Chairman GILMAN. Mr. Einhorn, we thank you for your patience and for being with us.

Pursuant to the earlier vote of the Committee, we will go to executive session. Before we do that, if there is no objection, I would ask that the Committee record be kept open it so that additional questions could be submitted in writing to Mr. Einhorn, and if that be the case, I hope you would respond expeditiously. Thank you again for being with us, Mr. Einhorn.

Mr. EINHORN. Thank you Mr. Chairman.

Chairman GILMAN. Now I am going to ask Mr. John Lauder to appear. We will have to clear the room, except for Committee Members, their designated staff, as well as witnesses and their staff.

[Whereupon, at 12:25 p.m., the Committee proceeded in executive session.]

APPENDIX

February 4, 1998

Opening Statement of Chairman Benjamin A. Gilman
Full Committee Hearing: Implementation of the U.S.-China Nuclear Cooperation Agreement

The hearing will come to order. Our witness today is the Honorable Robert Einhorn, who is the Deputy Assistant Secretary of State for Non-Proliferation.

Welcome, Mr. Einhorn.

The central question on the table today is how U.S. national interests are served by engaging in nuclear cooperation with China, and in particular, how U.S. non-proliferation objectives are fulfilled by such cooperation.

At a Full Committee hearing on October 11, 1997, the Committee spelled out its criteria for passing judgement on the U.S.-China Nuclear Cooperation Agreement. There were three basic points.

First, we said that the Administration must keep the Congress apprised of its intentions with regard to the Agreement. We urged them to brief regularly the Committee and lay out the Administration's rationale for implementing the Agreement before the October 1997 summit.

I believe the Administration has worked in good faith to meet those requests.

Second, we said that in order to implement the Agreement the Administration must make the required certification and report pursuant to the 1985 and 1990 laws that set conditions on any nuclear cooperation with China. We said that the certification must stand on its own and that the Administration must adhere to the letter of the law.

The President submitted the certification on January 12, 1998. In part, the purpose of today's hearing is to have the Administration make its case for the certification.

Until that case is heard, we will reserve judgement on whether the certification meets the requirements of the law.

Third, we said that, perhaps most importantly, the Administration would need to convince the Committee that now is the time to change the status quo with regard to nuclear cooperation with China.

And in that regard, I reiterate that it is not only China's <u>nuclear</u> non-proliferation record that is on trial. Clearly, Members must be convinced that China has stopped assisting Pakistan's nuclear weapons procurement program and Iran's efforts to develop an indigenous nuclear weapons capability.

But just as importantly Members need to know that China is engaging in responsible non-proliferation behavior across the board, including <u>all</u> weapons of mass destruction as well as conventional weapons.

In addition, Members need to understand why we have appeared to lower our non-proliferation standards by not insisting that China become a member of the Nuclear Suppliers Group (NSG) before we engage in nuclear cooperation with them.

And finally, Members need to be convinced beyond issuing pieces of paper that China has in place a fully functioning and effective export control system.

In that regard, we have been denied the ability to conduct post-shipment verification of our dual-use exports in China, a common practice for safeguarding our exports in many countries of the world, including Syria.

And it should be clear that we have noted the complete absence of any penalties or sanctions in the Chinese export control decrees.

It is in these areas that I do not believe the evidence supports engaging China in nuclear cooperation at this time.

Before proceeding further, there are a couple of procedural matters I would like to address.

We have worked out an arrangement with the Administration whereby we will remain in open session as long as Members have questions to address to Mr. Einhorn that can be answered in that forum.

When it is clear that all questions have been exhausted that can be addressed in open session, we will continue the hearing in closed session with Mr. Einhorn who will be joined by Mr. John Lauder, who is the Director of the Non-Proliferation Center at the Central Intelligence Agency.

House and Committee Rules require that we take a roll call vote with a majority of the Committee present to go into closed session. Therefore, I want to alert our witness and the Committee that when we have a majority of the Members present, I will entertain a motion to go into closed session. Assuming that vote allows us to go into closed session, we will then continue in open session until all Members have questions.

At this point, I have a series of unanimous consent requests to make.

I ask unanimous consent that a copy of the January 12, 1998, certification package submitted by the President be inserted in the record at the appropriate place.

I ask unanimous consent that a background memorandum prepared by the Congressional Research Service be placed at the appropriate place in the record. I would like to commend Shirley Kan at the CRS for her work in support of our Committee on this issue.

Further, I ask unanimous consent that a document entitled China's Non-Proliferation Words versus China's Nuclear Proliferation Deeds be inserted in the record at the appropriate place.

Mr. Hamilton, would you like to make an opening statement? Are there any other Members who would like to make an opening statement?

Mr. Einhorn, please proceed with your statement.

Sherrod Brown

Opening Statement
of Congressman Sherrod Brown
Committee on International Relations Hearing
on the U.S.-China Nuclear Cooperation Agreement
February 4, 1998

Mr. Chairman, I want to commend you for calling this important hearing, and would like to take this opportunity to remind the committee and our panelists that the U.S.-China Nuclear Cooperation Agreement has far wider ramifications than just its effects on the U.S.-China relationship. Over the years, China has engaged in irresponsible and destabilizing arms and technology sales which have increased tensions in various regions throughout Asia and the Middle East.

One of the most infamous examples of this worrisome behavior is China's previous sales of ring magnets and other nuclear technologies to Pakistan, a country which refuses to allow the International Atomic Energy Agency to inspect all of its nuclear facilities. Without the proper safeguards in place, these acts have clearly served to isolate and threaten India, one of America's emerging friends in South Asia.

Such sales cannot and should not be allowed to continue, and China claims to have stopped these transactions. By certifying Chinese compliance with the terms of this agreement, the Clinton Administration has taken China at its word. And yet, as recently as last June, the President's own Director of Central Intelligence stated that the People's Republic of China was Pakistan's principal supplier of equipment, material, and technology for its nuclear weapons program.

I would contend that U.S.-India relations are important enough and China's past record questionable enough to call for further monitoring of China's observance of its new commitments **before** this agreement is implemented. Such a delay is the right thing to do if we are to bolster security and development in South Asia and other parts of the world, and I would urge all my colleagues to seriously consider this option.

Thank you, Mr. Chairman.

Statement of Robert J. Einhorn
Deputy Assistant Secretary of State for Nonproliferation
Before the Committee on International Relations,
U.S. House of Representatives
February 4, 1998

Peaceful Nuclear Cooperation with China

Mr. Chairman,

Thank you for giving me the opportunity to testify before the Committee on the President's decision to submit to Congress the certifications and reports required by U.S. law to implement the 1985 U.S.-China Agreement for Peaceful Nuclear Cooperation.

China appears destined to be one of the 21st century's most powerful and influential countries. The security and prosperity of East Asia and indeed of the world at large will be affected significantly by how China defines and pursues its national interests. The United States, therefore, has a major stake in China being a responsible member of the international community, committed to stability in key regions of the world and to a range of other critical international norms, including the nonproliferation of weapons of mass destruction and missile delivery systems.

Nonproliferation has been one of the highest priorities of the Administration's engagement strategy with China, both because of the central importance of nonproliferation to U.S. security and because China -- as a nuclear weapon state, a Permanent Member of the U.N. Security Council, and a producer of a wide range of arms and sensitive technologies -- has become an increasingly indispensable player in international efforts to curb proliferation.

Another reason that nonproliferation has been high on the U.S.-China bilateral agenda is that China's past record in the area of proliferation has been a source of serious concern. For decades, China stood outside the international nonproliferation mainstream. In the 1960s, it even declared its support for the spread of nuclear weapons as a means of "breaking the hegemony of the superpowers." In the 1980s, it provided critical assistance to Pakistan's nuclear weapons program, assistance that clearly would have constituted a violation of the Nonproliferation Treaty had China been a party to the NPT at the time. Moreover, China or Chinese entities have sold missile equipment and technology, dual-use chemicals and production equipment, and advanced conventional arms to recipients in regions of tension and instability, primarily Iran and Pakistan.

An acute deficiency in China's nonproliferation record has been the absence of an effective, nationwide system of controls over sensitive exports. Even when Beijing has been willing to exercise restraint, its ability to do so has frequently been inadequate -- especially in the case of dual-use goods and technologies, including in the nuclear area.

Given these problems, the Administration has exerted a major effort to encourage a positive evolution in China's policies and practices. We saw a potentially promising opportunity to do so in negotiations on implementing the long-dormant U.S.-China Agreement for Peaceful Nuclear Cooperation. China has sought implementation of the 1985 Agreement in order to gain access to U.S. nuclear equipment and technology, which the Chinese apparently believe could make a significant contribution to their ambitious nuclear energy plans. Signed in 1985, the Agreement was approved by Congress on the condition that it could not be implemented until the President certified, in effect, that China was not assisting any non-nuclear weapon state to acquire nuclear weapons. In early 1995, as Members are aware, we entered into negotiations on steps that China could take in the area of nuclear nonproliferation to meet the requirements under U.S. law for activating the Peaceful Nuclear Cooperation Agreement.

The talks were carried out intensively for over two and a half years, concluding on October 29, 1997, the day of the White House meetings between President Clinton and President Jiang Zemin. We engaged at a variety of levels. Interagency teams of experts met regularly, and the President, Secretaries Christopher and Albright, and National Security Advisors Lake and Berger made nonproliferation a central focus of contacts with their Chinese counterparts. Throughout we consulted closely with Congress, particularly with Members and staff of this Committee.

We set high standards for meeting our legal requirements, and we pressed very hard. We pointed out to the Chinese the far-reaching benefits to both sides of reaching agreement, but we also reminded them that failure to address our concerns about Chinese nuclear cooperation with third countries would be a continuing impediment to stronger bilateral relations. This message was underlined in early 1996 when the transfer of ring magnets by a Chinese entity to Pakistan's unsafeguarded uranium enrichment program became a major and high-level irritant between the two governments and a hold was placed on all Export-Import Bank loans to China during the three-month period needed to resolve the controversy.

U.S. goals in the nuclear nonproliferation talks were carefully chosen to satisfy -- and in some cases exceed -- the requirements of U.S. law to implement the 1985 Agreement. Our goals were: (1) to terminate Chinese assistance to Pakistan's unsafeguarded nuclear facilities and nuclear explosive program, (2) to curtail Chinese cooperation with Iran's safeguarded nuclear program, (3) to establish an effective Chinese nuclear and nuclear-related dual-use export control system, and (4) to obtain Chinese participation in multilateral nuclear export control efforts. We achieved important results in each of these areas.

- China made a commitment in May 1996 not to provide assistance to unsafeguarded nuclear facilities, in Pakistan or anywhere else. The Chinese appear to be taking this pledge very seriously. We are not aware of any transfers of equipment or material by Chinese entities to Pakistan's unsafeguarded nuclear program since the pledge was made. From recent Chinese official directives and statements, we are confident that the Chinese share our understanding that "assistance" covers transfers of technology and information (not just hardware) and that the pledge precludes assistance both to unsafeguarded fuel cycle facilities and nuclear explosive programs in non-nuclear weapon states. We have discussed with Chinese officials specific cases of potential concern involving contacts between Chinese entities and elements associated with Pakistan's nuclear weapons program, and will continue to do so if the need arises. But our current information indicates that China appears to be acting consistently with its May 1996 commitment.

- China has agreed to phase out its nuclear cooperation with Iran. Even though Chinese nuclear cooperation with Iran has been limited to the peaceful uses of nuclear energy and has been under IAEA safeguards, we urged China (as we have urged all other nuclear suppliers) to refrain from any such cooperation because of our concerns that

Iran is seeking nuclear weapons and our belief that even safeguarded cooperation could contribute to that effort. China has suspended the sale of two nuclear power reactors to Iran, canceled the transfer of a uranium conversion facility that could have provided an essential element of Iran's nuclear weapons program, and turned down Iranian requests for other sensitive equipment and technology. It has also provided a clear assurance that it is not going to engage in new nuclear cooperation with Iran and that it will complete its few existing projects -- which are not of proliferation concern -- within a relatively short period of time.

- China is putting in place for the first time a comprehensive, nationwide system of nuclear and nuclear-related dual-use export controls. This system is reflected in several specific measures that China has implemented. In May 1997, China's State Council issued a directive to all government agencies and non-governmental entities on the control of nuclear-related exports. It highlighted the policy of not assisting unsafeguarded nuclear facilities and specifically covered exchanges of technical personnel and information. In June 1997, the Chinese published an interim list of nuclear-related dual-use items substantively identical to the Nuclear Suppliers Group's dual-use list. In September 1997, the State Council promulgated nuclear export control regulations, published a nuclear control list substantively identical to the trigger list used by the Nuclear Suppliers Group, and subsequently committed to promulgate final dual-use regulations by mid-1998 which we expect to include a final version of the nuclear-related dual-use control list.

- China became a member of the NPT Exporters Committee (Zangger Committee) in October 1997, the first time China has joined a multilateral nonproliferation export control regime. Committee membership will both enhance China's export control expertise and strengthen its commitment to nonproliferation norms and practices. At the October meeting, the Chinese representative issued a comprehensive statement of China's nuclear export control policy that made explicit Beijing's adherence to key nuclear export control principles, including the need for supplier governments to have the authority to deny the export of items not found on control lists if the export could contribute to proliferation (i.e., catch-all controls).

The recent steps the Chinese have taken and the new assurances they have provided meet our negotiating goals and, more importantly, satisfy the standards set by the Congress for implementing the 1985 Agreement. The commitments China has undertaken -- including on not assisting unsafeguarded nuclear facilities and on phasing out nuclear cooperation with Iran -- are explicit and mutually understood and set clear benchmarks to evaluate Chinese behavior. But the progress we have seen involves more than words, more than commitments on paper. We have already begun to see concrete actions -- in terms of sales to third countries rejected or canceled, detailed regulations and control lists adopted and publicized, and active participation in international regimes initiated.

Moreover, the steps noted above should be viewed in the context of other developments, primarily during the 1990s, that demonstrate China's growing acceptance of nuclear nonproliferation norms -- including adherence to the NPT and support for its indefinite and unconditional extension, termination of nuclear testing and signature of the Comprehensive Test Ban Treaty, support for a Fissile Material Cutoff Treaty, support for the strengthened safeguards system of the IAEA, and the helpful role played in achieving the Agreed Framework with North Korea.

Taken together, these various steps and developments constitute a marked, positive shift in China's nuclear nonproliferation policies and practices. On the basis of this record, and taking carefully into account the specific requirements of U.S. law, the President announced on October 29, 1997 that he would submit to Congress the certifications and report necessary to implement the 1985 Agreement. He signed the certification package on January 12 of this year. It is now sitting before the Congress for the 30 continuous legislative days required before the Agreement can be implemented.

Implementation of the 1985 Agreement will bring important benefits for the United States.

It will provide an effective means of encouraging China to live up to the nuclear nonproliferation commitments it has recently made. It is necessary to point out, in this connection, that the 1985 U.S.-PRC Agreement will make China eligible to receive U.S. nuclear exports; it does not guarantee that China will receive them. Under our nuclear licensing procedures, individual transactions will have to be approved on a case-by-case basis and each license is subject to a thorough interagency review process. If the

Chinese do not abide by their assurances, we can withhold approval of new licenses and even revoke previously-approved licenses.

Implementation will therefore give China continuing incentives to fulfill its obligations. We will be monitoring Chinese behavior closely. Given the close historical ties between China and Pakistan and the challenge Beijing faces in implementing its new export control system, it is certainly conceivable that cases will arise that raise questions. If and when we encounter problems or uncertainties, we will not hesitate to raise them with Beijing. With the 1985 Agreement in effect -- and prospects for continued cooperation potentially at risk -- the Chinese will have a strong stake in being responsive to our inquiries and in taking prompt, corrective steps to prevent or stop any activities inconsistent with China's policies and commitments. Failure to proceed with implementation, on the other hand, would deprive us of the best vehicle we have for promoting cooperative and conscientious follow-up on China's undertakings.

Activating the Agreement will also give us the most promising basis for making further progress in the nonproliferation area. The U.S. will use the Agreement and its broad provisions for consultations, specifically in Article 8, as a framework for continuing to engage China on such matters as export controls and China's policies and practices toward nuclear cooperation with other countries.

There are already indications of how the Agreement can pave the way for further progress. During President Jiang's visit in October, the Department of Energy and China's State Planning Commission concluded an Agreement of Intent on cooperation concerning peaceful uses of nuclear technology. It provides for government-to-government cooperation in nuclear export controls, nuclear materials control and accountancy, physical protection of nuclear materials and facilities, international nuclear safeguards, nuclear reactor safety, and other areas of mutual interest. These are matters of critical importance to U.S. national security. Some limited cooperation has occurred in these areas between U.S. and Chinese national laboratories, as an agreement for nuclear cooperation is not required for minor cooperation of this nature. However, Beijing has held that the Agreement for Peaceful Nuclear Cooperation was needed first to provide an appropriate foundation for official government-to-government cooperation. The Agreement should also provide impetus to U.S.-Chinese cooperation in reducing the enrichment level of research reactor fuel -- an international effort of long standing which seeks to reduce the amount of highly enriched uranium in international commerce.

Proceeding with the 1985 Agreement will also put us in a stronger position to press for progress on non-nuclear nonproliferation issues -- chemical, missile, and advanced conventional arms -- where serious problems remain in China's policies and practices. Implementing the Agreement will demonstrate to the Chinese that, if they make hard choices and modify their behavior to bring it into line with international norms, mutually beneficial areas of cooperation will open up. It is important now that the Chinese make some similarly hard choices in the area of China's non-nuclear cooperation with third countries. But if -- after China has met our conditions for implementing the 1985 Agreement -- we do not keep our end of the bargain, they will be reluctant to accept our proposals in other areas.

While improving China's policies and practices in nuclear nonproliferation was the main objective of our dialogue with China on conditions for implementing the 1985 Agreement, we have also been aware of the commercial benefits likely to result from implementation. China intends to make nuclear power one of its major energy sources in the 21st century. Indeed, China provides the fastest growing nuclear power market in the world today. A variety of foreign nuclear reactor vendors are eager to sell their products to China, and in fact China has already negotiated arrangements to purchase reactors from France, Russia, and Canada. However, the Chinese clearly hold in high regard the safety, design, and performance of U.S. nuclear equipment and technology and have made plain their interest in cooperating with American partners.

The sales of equipment and technology under the Agreement will be commercial transactions between the Chinese Government and U.S. private industry. It is therefore difficult at this stage to predict or quantify the economic activity that would be generated by providing U.S. firms access to China's market. But it is clear that the market in China for nuclear reactors alone is a multi-billion dollar one, and so we would expect the benefits in terms of balance of trade and industrial job creation at home to be substantial.

Moreover, given the highly safe and environmentally sound character of advanced U.S. nuclear reactor designs, American firms' access to the China market can also be expected to serve U.S. international reactor safety and environmental goals. U.S. reactor sales will help China reduce its reliance on fossil-fuel electricity-generating plants and therefore significantly limit the huge projected growth in China's greenhouse gas emissions.

The Administration believes that the arguments for proceeding promptly with implementation of the Agreement are powerful. At the same time, we have listened carefully to the concerns voiced by Members of Congress, including members of this Committee, in the floor debate on this matter in early November. Members posed some serious questions about moving ahead now with China on nuclear cooperation, and I would like briefly to address three of the questions most frequently raised.

First, a number of Members ask whether the Chinese can be trusted to live up to their new commitments in light of the unsatisfactory record of past behavior.

The Administration is fully conscious of the history of this matter, including most notably China's assistance to Pakistan's unsafeguarded nuclear program even after signing the peaceful nuclear cooperation agreement in 1985. But the issue before us is not the historical record; it is whether China is now abiding by its commitments and will do so in the future.

In addressing an issue of such importance, we must not rely simply on assurances; we need deeds, not just words. And the deeds we have observed so far by China -- its termination of certain activities with third countries, its implementation of export controls, its participation in international regimes -- are encouraging. They appear to reflect a level of seriousness and commitment we did not see before.

Notwithstanding these positive signs of change, we approach implementation of the Agreement with the same healthy skepticism we would bring to any such international undertaking. President Reagan's advice to "trust but verify" is certainly appropriate. So we will monitor very carefully China's activities with other countries and take appropriate steps to address any problematic behavior. The Chinese are aware that any actions inconsistent with their nuclear nonproliferation assurances would jeopardize nuclear cooperation with the United States.

Second, a number of Members point out China's problematic record in missile, chemical, and conventional arms exports and suggest that we make implementation of the nuclear cooperation agreement conditional upon improvement in China's export policies and practices not just in the nuclear area but in these non-nuclear areas as well.

It should be noted, in this connection, that we have made gains with the Chinese in recent years in the non-nuclear area. For example, we believe China is abiding by its October 1994 pledge not to sell MTCR-class ground-to-ground missiles. China became an original party to the Chemical Weapons Convention and put in place a system of chemical export controls. And recently the Chinese confirmed to Secretary Cohen what they had told Secretary Albright earlier -- that they will stop transfers to Iran of anti-ship cruise missiles and related production technology.

The Administration recognizes, however, that progress with the Chinese in the non-nuclear areas has lagged behind progress on nuclear issues. While no longer selling complete MTCR-class missiles, China continues to transfer missile components and technology, especially to Pakistan and Iran. Despite some recent steps to regulate the activities of certain Chinese chemical companies more effectively, we are still aware of cooperation between Chinese entities and questionable Iranian buyers in dual-use chemicals and production equipment, and we still believe that China's chemical export controls in this area are not sufficiently comprehensive or effective.

A major focus of the Administration's engagement policy with China in the period ahead will be to press for substantial improvements in these non-nuclear areas. But we cannot support linking implementation of the nuclear agreement to further progress on these other issues. The prerequisites for proceeding to implement the 1985 Agreement -- as drafted by Congress and embodied in law -- are clear. They require performance in terms of China's nuclear nonproliferation policies and practices. To insist now on additional steps in other areas would amount to moving the goalposts and going beyond what our law requires. Prospects for succeeding with this strategy are remote. In seeking to change the terms of the deal, we would make it more difficult to achieve further progress and could even put in jeopardy some of the concrete gains achieved to date.

Third, some Members, while acknowledging positive signs in China's recent behavior, recommend that we postpone implementation of the Agreement for another year or so while we accumulate a better "track record" to evaluate China's willingness and ability to abide by its commitments.

The Administration understands the desire to see a track record. But in a real sense, we have already acquired a substantial track record. We have been focusing very heavily on China's nuclear export activities in recent years, and since May 1996 have especially scrutinized its pledge not to assist unsafeguarded nuclear facilities. As I indicated earlier, the Chinese appear to be taking their commitments very seriously. When questions have arisen, we have pursued them vigorously in diplomatic channels. But there is no basis so far to conclude that China has not abided by its commitments.

It would be futile to put off implementation until all questions and uncertainties about Chinese behavior ceased to exist. Uncertainties inevitably will continue to arise. It is in the nature of intelligence gathering and in the often-ambiguous nature of the activities we are focusing on. Moreover, such uncertainties are not peculiar to China. They would arise, to a greater or lesser extent, in monitoring the activities of virtually any significant producing and exporting country.

Still, it is essential to resolve such uncertainties and, especially in the case of China, to assess whether it is meeting its obligations. But the best way to resolve any concerns or uncertainties is not to postpone implementation. Rather it is to proceed with implementation, and to use the incentives and opportunities that the Agreement provides -- namely, China's stake in nuclear cooperation with the U.S. and the many bilateral interactions that the Agreement ensures -- to press for answers to our questions and insist on scrupulous compliance.

It is important to recognize that there is a substantial risk in putting off implementation in the hope of gaining a more complete track record. China is now in the process of making major decisions about its future nuclear power program. As much as it may prefer to cooperate with American partners, it clearly has other options -- and it cannot wait for us much longer. If we were now to postpone implementation, China might well write us out of its future nuclear plans and opt to buy from others -- and those other suppliers would certainly not drive as hard a nonproliferation bargain as we have. Not only would we lose the commercial benefits, but we would risk losing some of the nonproliferation gains we have already achieved -- especially on Iran -- and we would deprive ourselves of an important continuing source of leverage to influence Chinese behavior.

Mr. Chairman, we know that Members of this Committee attach great importance to Chinese compliance with international nonproliferation norms. Therefore, we suggest that, in considering the question of implementing the 1985 Agreement, Members ask themselves which approach would be most effective in promoting such compliance -- proceeding now with implementation or further postponing implementation until China makes additional progress on non-nuclear issues and until we have a more complete track record of improved Chinese behavior in the nuclear field.

The Administration is confident that the first approach is the best way to advance our nonproliferation goals with China -- both to consolidate the progress already achieved in the nuclear area and to persuade the Chinese to strengthen their uneven performance in the missile, chemical, and conventional arms areas. The record of recent years demonstrates clearly, in our view, that the most promising means of dealing with the Chinese on these issues is through tough, frank, persistent engagement, using a combination of carrots and sticks. Implementing the 1985 Agreement now -- in full conformance with the requirements of U.S. law -- will provide us an essential vehicle for pursuing this effort. It will give the Chinese continuing incentives to make further progress on our nonproliferation agenda and to deal promptly and effectively with any questions that may arise in the nuclear area.

The alternative course of further delay would weaken our ability to press our case. Having moved the goalposts after the Chinese had taken hard decisions to meet our conditions, we would have a difficult time inducing them to do more. And having failed to lock in the gains already made, we would risk some unraveling, especially in areas where we have persuaded the Chinese to go beyond their international legal obligations.

In 1985 and again in 1990, Congress passed laws making U.S. nuclear cooperation with China conditional upon improvement in Chinese nuclear nonproliferation policies and practices. This Administration, recognizing the difficulty of encouraging Chinese movement in this highly sensitive area, saw the opportunity to use those laws as tools to promote an outcome that would not only advance important nonproliferation objectives, but also would enable the U.S. and China to reap the commercial and energy benefits of nuclear cooperation and strengthen their growing bilateral ties. The tools have been effective. We have witnessed a demonstrable improvement in China's approach to nuclear nonproliferation -- an improvement measured in concrete steps actually taken, not just promises about future behavior. But it would be a mistake to expect those tools to do more than they were originally designed to do. We could lose what they have already helped us to achieve.

In the interest of advancing U.S. nonproliferation goals -- as well as of promoting America's overall interest in building a mutually advantageous relationship with China that is firmly based on a shared respect for international norms such as nonproliferation -- we ask that the Committee join us in supporting the prompt implementation of the 1985 Agreement.

Prerequisites for Implementation of the U.S.-PRC Agreement for Peaceful Nuclear Cooperation

On December 16, 1985, a Joint Resolution entered into force approving the U.S.-PRC Agreement for Peaceful Nuclear Cooperation. (P.L. 99-183, S.J. Res. 238) However, this joint resolution of approval provided that no export license may be issued and no approval for the transfer or retransfer of any nuclear material, facilities, or components subject to the Agreement shall be given until the expiration of a period of thirty days of continuous session of Congress after the President has submitted the following certifications and reports to the Congress:

-- First, the President has to certify to Congress that the reciprocal arrangements made pursuant to Article 8 of the Agreement (for exchanges of information and visits) have been designed to be effective in ensuring that any nuclear material, facilities, or components provided under the Agreement shall be utilized solely for intended purposes as set forth in the Agreement.

-- Second, the President has to certify to Congress that the PRC has provided additional information concerning its nuclear nonproliferation policies and that, based on this and all other information available to the United States Government, the PRC is not in violation of paragraph (2) of section 129 of the Atomic Energy Act of 1954. (The relevant portions of section 129(2) involve nuclear trade restrictions against nations that (1) have assisted, encouraged, or induced a nonnuclear-weapon state to engage in activities involving nuclear material and having direct significance for the acquisition of nuclear weapons and have failed to take sufficient steps to terminate such behavior, or (2) have entered into an agreement for the transfer of reprocessing equipment, materials, or technology to a nonnuclear-weapon state.)

-- Third, the President has to certify to Congress that the obligation to consider favorably a request to carry out activities described in Article 5(2) of the Agreement shall not prejudice the decision of the United States to approve or disapprove such a request. (Article 5(2) obligates the parties to "consider favorably" any request to carry out certain activities described in that article, i.e. (1) enrichment above twenty percent, (2) alteration in form or content, or (3) a change in storage location, where such activities involve nuclear material subject to the Agreement.)

-- Fourth, the President has to submit to the Speaker of the House of Representatives and the Chairman of the Committee on Foreign Relations of the Senate a report detailing the history and current developments in the nonproliferation policies and practices of the PRC. (The report shall be submitted in unclassified form with a classified addendum.)

In February 1990, Congress imposed three conditions on nuclear-related trade with the PRC as part of the Foreign Relations Authorization Act for Fiscal Years 1990 and 1991. (P.L.

101-246) The conditions established in this Act, like those of the 1985 resolution of approval, restricted export licenses and transfer/retransfer approvals for nuclear material, facilities, or components subject to the Agreement. However, they also restricted (1) Department of Commerce licenses for the export to the PRC (for use in a nuclear production or utilization facility) of nuclear-related dual-use items controlled under section 309(c) of the Nuclear Nonproliferation Act of 1978 and (2) Department of Energy specific authorization under section 57b.(2) of the Atomic Energy Act for assistance in any activities with respect to the PRC relating to the use of nuclear energy. The three conditions imposed in 1990 are:

-- The President must certify to Congress that the PRC has provided clear and unequivocal assurances to the United States that it is not assisting and will not assist any nonnuclear-weapon state, either directly or indirectly, in acquiring nuclear explosive devices or the materials and components for such devices.

-- The President must make the certifications and submit the report required in the resolution of approval of the U.S.-PRC Agreement for Cooperation. The effect of this repetition of the requirements in the Joint Resolution is to extend those requirements to Department of Commerce-licensed dual-use exports and Department of Energy-approved specific authorizations to transfer nuclear technology.

-- The President must report to Congress either (1) that the Government of the PRC has made progress on a program of political reform throughout the country, including Tibet, which includes of lifting martial law; halting executions and other reprisals against individuals for the nonviolent expression of their political beliefs; release of political prisoners; increased respect for internationally recognized human rights, including freedom of expression, the press, assembly, and association; and permitting a freer flow of information, including an end to the jamming of Voice of America, and greater access to foreign journalists; or (2) that it is in the national interest of the United States to terminate the restrictions on nuclear-related trade.

CHINA'S NUCLEAR AND NUCLEAR-RELATED DUAL-USE EXPORT CONTROLS

State Council Decree

In May 1997, China's State Council issued a Circular on Strict Implementation of China's Nuclear Export Policy which covered the export of nuclear and nuclear-related dual-use items on an interim basis. This directive:

- Applies to all governmental and nongovernmental entities in China.
- States that nuclear materials, nuclear equipment and related technology, non-nuclear materials for reactors, and nuclear-related dual-use equipment, materials and technologies on China's export list may not be supplied to or used in facilities not under IAEA safeguards.
- Covers technology in all forms, including exchanges of personnel and information.
- Requires exporters of nuclear-related dual-use items to non-NPT countries: (I) to seek prior confirmation from China's Atomic Energy Authority of the IAEA safeguards status of nuclear facilities in the recipient country; and (ii) to seek end-user certificates from the importing government along with assurances that the relevant equipment or cooperation will not be retransferred to unsafeguarded nuclear facilities.
- The associated control list (issued in June 1997) is substantively identical to the dual-use control list adopted by the Nuclear Suppliers Group (published in IAEA INFCIRC 254, Part II).

Nuclear Export Control Regulations

In September 1997, China issued nuclear export control regulations and an associated control list. These regulations:

- Apply to all governmental and non-governmental entities in China.
- Provide that all nuclear exports are under the control of the State Atomic Energy Agency which will examine all nuclear export applications and refer them to other appropriate agencies as necessary (i.e. MOFTEC, SSTC, MFA).
- Control nuclear materials, nuclear equipment and related technology, non-nuclear materials for reactors, related information and technology and personnel exchanges.
- Include a control list substantively identical to the "trigger list" adopted by the Nuclear Suppliers Group (published in IAEA INFCIRC 254, Part I).

- State that only units designated by the State Council are permitted to engage in such exports.
- Give the Chinese Government the right to suspend exports if the recipient country violates its commitments or there is a danger of nuclear proliferation.
- Require recipient governments to provide assurances of peaceful use, IAEA safeguards, no retransfer to third parties without Chinese government approval, and physical protection of nuclear material.
- Establish authority for taking criminal, civil or administrative actions against violators of the regulations.
- Finally, in its statement at the Zangger Committee, China stressed that its export controls include a "catch-all" authority whereby exports which violate the export control principles, or pose a proliferation risk, whether or not they are on a control list, will be denied export licenses.

Zangger Committee Membership

On October 16, 1997, China joined the NPT Exporters Committee, also known as the Zangger Committee, which represents China's first membership in a multilateral export control regime. Ambassador Li Changhe of the Chinese Permanent Mission in Vienna delivered a prepared statement at the October meeting which outlined in detail China's nuclear and nuclear-related dual-use export control policies and practices. His statement set forth the basis and content of Chinese nuclear export controls, and he stressed that China's nuclear export control system is based on three basic principles: (1) serving peaceful purposes only; (2) accepting IAEA safeguards; (3) forbidding transfer to any third country without China's consent.

Li also made clear that China's policy of not assisting unsafeguarded nuclear facilities extends to activities related to nuclear explosive devices, and that China strictly prohibits any exchange of nuclear weapons related technology and information with other countries. In another key pronouncement, Li affirmed that Chinese government departments have the right to deny the export of an item not on a control list if there is reason to believe that the export might contribute to nuclear proliferation. Such "catch-all" controls have become an important feature of an effective nationwide WMD export control system.

Nuclear-related Dual-Use Export Control Regulations

Chinese authorities have stated that they will issue formal nuclear-related dual-use export control regulations by mid-1998. Ambassador Li, in his statement to the Zangger Committee, confirmed that the control list associated with these regulations will be based on the Nuclear Suppliers Groups dual-use control list, as defined in INFCIRC 254, Part II (as were China's interim dual-use controls discussed above). Until the formal dual-use regulations are issued, the Interim Directive controls nuclear-related dual-use exports.

China's Record on Nuclear Arms Control and Nonproliferation

On January 12, 1998, President Clinton made the certifications required by Public Laws 99-183 and 101-246 for implementation of the 1985 US/China Agreement for Peaceful Nuclear Cooperation. These certifications were forwarded to the Congress for the statutory period of Congressional review along with the "Unclassified Report to Congress on the Nonproliferation Policies and Practices of the People's Republic of China." A classified version of that report was also forwarded to the Congress. Those reports traced the positive evolution of Chinese policy with respect to arms control, nuclear nonproliferation and export controls, and a developing Chinese appreciation for the value of multilateral nuclear export control efforts.

The following examples of positive developments in Chinese policy are drawn from the reports to Congress and demonstrate why the Administration believes that the legislative requirements for implementation of the US/China Agreement have been met.

- Although initially critical of the Nonproliferation Treaty (NPT), the cornerstone of the nuclear nonproliferation regime, China adhered to the NPT in 1992.

- In 1994, Beijing played a constructive role with North Korea in promoting the October 1994 U.S.-DPRK Agreed Framework, under which the North agreed to freeze and eventually eliminate its nuclear weapons program.

- Also in 1994, China joined with the United States in calling for the negotiation of a multilateral agreement banning the production of fissile material for nuclear weapons and other nuclear explosive devices.

- In 1995, China supported the successful effort to indefinitely extend the NPT.

- In 1996, China ceased testing nuclear weapons and signed the Comprehensive Test Ban Treaty.

- On May 11, 1996, China committed not to provide assistance to unsafeguarded nuclear facilities.

- With respect to nuclear export controls, China issued a State Council Circular in May 1997 providing interim controls over nuclear and nuclear-related dual-use exports. In September, China promulgated detailed nuclear export control regulations which incorporated the internationally-agreed "trigger list" of the Nuclear Suppliers Group (NSG). In October, China announced that it would promulgate formal nuclear-related dual-use export controls by mid-1998. These controls will be based on the list of dual-use items controlled by the NSG.

- On October 16, 1997, China joined the NPT Exporters Committee, also known as the Zangger Committee, as a full member. This is the first instance in which China has participated as a full member in a multilateral export control group dedicated to the nonproliferation of weapons of mass destruction. During the October meeting, China released a comprehensive statement outlining its nuclear export control policies and practices.

- China has terminated its plans to provide power reactors and a uranium conversion facility to Iran, as well as other facilities that might have significantly contributed to a nuclear infrastructure supporting Iranian nuclear weapons ambitions.

- China has provided a clear assurance that it is not going to engage in new nuclear cooperation with Iran, and that it will terminate all existing cooperation within a relatively short period of time.

- In 1997, China joined with other members of the IAEA in negotiating and then recommending that the IAEA Board of Governors adopt a new safeguards arrangement that will strengthen the IAEA's ability to detect undeclared nuclear activities in states with comprehensive safeguards agreements.

中华人民共和国常驻维也纳联合国和其他国际组织代表团

THE PERMANENT MISSION OF THE PEOPLE'S REPUBLIC OF CHINA
TO THE UNITED NATIONS AND OTHER INTERNATIONAL ORGANIZATIONS IN VIENNA

(Translation)

Statement by Ambassador Li Changhe Of the Chinese Permanent Mission in Vienna at the Meeting of the Zangger Committee

16 October 1997

Mr. Chairman,

I am very pleased to attend this meeting of the Zangger Committee to represent China as its full member for the first time. China supports the general goals of the Committee, appreciates the positive role the Committee has played in preventing nuclear proliferation, and stands ready to conduct regular consultations with other member countries of the Committee of issues of nuclear non-proliferation and export control with a view to making joint efforts to prevent proliferation of nuclear weapons.

Mr. Chairman,

The recently concluded 15th national Congress of the Communist Party of China has reiterated that economic development is the focus in the work of the whole Party and the whole nation, and emphasized that China's modernization drive requires a long-term peaceful international environment. Therefore, China will continue its pursuit of an independent foreign policy of peace, and work for maintaining regional and global peace, stability and prosperity . To prevent weapons of mass destruction of all descriptions, including nuclear weapons, is an important component of this foreign policy of peace.

As a member of the International Atomic Energy Agency and State Party to the Non-proliferation Treaty, China adheres to the policy that it does not advocate, encourage or engage in proliferation of nuclear weapons nor assist other countries in developing nuclear weapons. For many years the Chinese Government has exercised strict and effective control over nuclear and nuclear-related export, including exchanges of personnel and information, and has abided by the following three principles: 1) serving peaceful purposes only; 2) accepting IAEA safeguards; 3) forbidding transfer to any third country without China's consent. With regard to any nuclear export, the recipient government is always requested to provide to the Chinese side an assurance in writing to acknowledge the above three principles and the export can proceed only after approval by relevant Chinese authorities.

In actual implementation, China has always administered nuclear export and nuclear cooperation through a management which combines laws, regulations and administrative decrees. The State Council and the competent authorities of various industries have laid down strict and specific regulations on nuclear export and nuclear cooperation, and strictly prohibit any exchange of nuclear weapons related technology and information with other countries. Such management falls in line with China's national conditions and has proved effective in practice.

Mr. Chairman,

Along with the deepening of the reform and opening-up and the gradual development from the planned economy to a socialist market economy, the Chinese Government has in the recent period of time taken a series of positive measures on the basis of the existing management to further strengthen and improve the mechanism for nuclear export control. Our efforts in this regard are still going on. The following is my detailed introduction in this regard.

I. In May 1997, the State Council of China promulgated the Circular on Strict Implementation of China's Nuclear Export Policy, which provides that the nuclear materials, nuclear equipment and related technology, as well as non-nuclear materials for reactors, and nuclear-related dual-use equipment, materials and relevant technologies on China's export list must not be supplied to or used in nuclear facilities not under IAEA safeguards. No agency or company is allowed to conduct cooperation or exchange of personnel and technological data with nuclear facilities not under IAEA safeguards. I would like to point that the above regulations are applicable not only to nuclear facilities not under safeguards, but also to all activities related to nuclear explosive devices.

II. The Circular also provides that in conducting the above-mentioned trade or activities in nuclear facilities with a non-signatory to NPT, any Chinese agency or company should seek prior confirmation from the State Atomic Energy Authority whether or not the nuclear facilities in question are under IAEA safeguards and ask for in advance certificate of end-use from competent authorities of the recipient government and an assurance that the equipment so imported or cooperation so conducted will not be transferred to nuclear facilities not under safeguards. In case of no nuclear facilities are involved, competent authorities of the recipient government are required to provide in advance a reasonable and reliable end-use certificate for the equipment so imported and an assurance that the equipment so imported or cooperation so conducted will not be transferred to nuclear facilities not under safeguards. Such export or activities of cooperation can not proceed until confirmation and approval are granted by China's Ministry of Foreign Affairs, Ministry of Foreign Trade and Economic Cooperation (MOFTEC) and the State Atomic Energy Authority with regard to the above-mentioned certificates. Annexed to the Circular is the control list of dual-use items which is identical to Party II of INFCIRC 254. The promulgation of the above regulations has guaranteed China's effective control on nuclear-related dual-use items before the promulgation of relevant laws and regulations on the export control of such items.

III. The Circular has been formulated by China's State Council as empowered by the Constitution and is legally binding. All the departments concerned should comply with it and the supportive detailed rules for implementation will be formulated, no unit, companies or laboratories can be excepted.

IV. In order to transform relevant policies and regulation into law, China's State Council promulgated last September the Regulations on Nuclear Export Control, establishing in the form of law the three principles governing China's nuclear export and the policy not provide assistance to nuclear facilities not under safeguards.

1. The Regulations provide that nuclear export is monopolized by units designated by the State Council. No other or individual is allowed to engage in such export. A licensing system is applied to the nuclear export by the State, i.e. all the items and their technologies on the "Nuclear Export Control List" should apply for an export license. The control list is the same as Part I of the INFCIRC 254.

2. The Regulations provide that the State Atomic Energy Authority shall examine nuclear export applications. If the approved application involves nuclear materials, it shall be referred to the Commission of Science, Technology and Industry for National Defense for re-examination; if it involves other materials, it shall be referred to the MOFTEC for re-

examination. Any nuclear export which has a bearing on state security, social and public interests or foreign policy, the Ministry of Foreign Affairs should be consulted; when necessary, such export should be further reported to the State Council for approval. After approval, the MOFTEC will issue an export license.

3. The Regulations provide that if the recipient government should violate its commitment made under these Regulations, or if there is an imminent danger of nuclear proliferation, the department concerned of the Chinese Government has the right to suspend such export.

4. The Regulations provide that any violation of the Regulations is liable to punishment by law.

The Regulations are not only distributed and made known to all the relevant units through regular channels, but also published by the People's Daily which has the largest circulation in China and other newspapers and periodicals so as to ensure the broadest possible public awareness. On September 15, the spokesman of the Foreign Ministry of the Chinese Government made a special statement to comprehensively and authoritatively expound the policy of the Chinese Government on the issue of nuclear non-proliferation and nuclear export control in connection with the promulgation of the Regulations on Nuclear Export Control.

V. Relevant departments of China are stepping up their efforts to complete the export control regulations on the nuclear-related dual use items. The control list of the regulations will be the same as Part II of INFCIR 254 on dual use items. The export of all the items on the list will be subject of strict examination procedures. In addition, if the relevant department of the Government has reason to believe that the export of some item may possibly cause nuclear proliferation, even though the item may not be listed, the department concerned has the right to ban or suspend such an export. The regulations will be completed by mid-1998.

The promulgation and implementation of the above-mentioned regulations will basically systemize China's laws on nuclear export.

Mr. Chairman,

The prevention of nuclear proliferation is a long and arduous task which calls for the joint efforts of the international community. At the same time, the Chinese side wishes to emphasize that the prevention of nuclear proliferation should in no way affect or hinder the normal nuclear cooperation for peaceful uses among countries, let alone be used as an excuse for discrimination and even application of willful sanctions against developing countries. The prevention of nuclear proliferation and peaceful uses of nuclear energy constitute the two sides of one coin. The two promote each other and neither can be dispensed with. This is the consistent policy of China. The Chinese Government is ready to make unremitting efforts with other countries for the common development of both nuclear non-proliferation and peaceful uses of nuclear energy.

Thank you, Mr. Chairman.

THE WHITE HOUSE

WASHINGTON

January 12, 1998

Dear Mr. Chairman:

I am writing to you with respect to sections (b)(1) and (b)(2) of Public Law 99-183, relating to the approval and implementation of the Agreement for Nuclear Cooperation Between the United States and the People's Republic of China, and with respect to section 902(a)(6)(B) of Public Law 101-246. The sections of Public Law 99-183 cited above require certifications to the Congress and a report to the Speaker of the House of Representatives and the Chairman of the Committee on Foreign Relations of the Senate before exports or retransfers to China under the Agreement may begin. Sections 902(a)6(B)(i), (ii) and (iii) of Public Law 101-246 require a certification to the Congress and report to the Congress before terminating the suspensions and automatic disapprovals of nuclear cooperation with China.

I have made the certifications pursuant to section (b)(1) of Public Law 99-183 and section 902(a)(6)(B)(i) of Public Law 101-246, a copy of which is enclosed. The certifications pursuant to section (b)(1) of Public Law 99-183 satisfy the condition under section 902(a)(6)(B)(ii). Submitted herewith, in accordance with the requirements of section (b)(2) of Public Law 99-183, is a report in unclassified form detailing the history and current developments in the nonproliferation policies, practices and assurances of the People's Republic of China. Because of the information controls that apply to the classified report, I am transmitting it by separate letter to the House Permanent Select Committee on Intelligence and the Senate Select Committee on Intelligence.

In accordance with Public Law 99-183, I have certified as to three matters:

(A) That the reciprocal arrangements made pursuant to Article 8 of the Agreement have been designed to be effective in ensuring that any nuclear material, facilities or components provided under the Agreement shall be utilized solely for intended peaceful purposes as set forth in the Agreement.

50-151 98-3

The arrangements for exchanges of information and visits are provided for in a Memorandum of Understanding initialed on June 23, 1987. Side notes on protection of business confidential information were signed on October 22, 1997. These documents, along with a detailed explanation of my certification, are enclosed. These arrangements will provide the United States with the right to obtain all the information necessary to maintain an inventory of the items subject to the Agreement. This will include information on the operation of facilities subject to the Agreement, the isotopic composition, physical form and quantity of material subject to the Agreement and the places where items subject to the Agreement are used or kept. The arrangements also provide the United States with the right to confirm through on-site visits the use of all items subject to the Agreement. Finally, the arrangements apply as long as the provisions of Article 8(2) of the Agreement continue in effect, that is, as long as items subject to the Agreement remain in China's territory or under its jurisdiction or control. My determination that these arrangements have been designed to be effective in ensuring that items provided under the Agreement are utilized for intended peaceful purposes is based on consideration of a range of factors, including the limited scope of nuclear cooperation permitted under the Agreement, U.S. export-control procedures that will apply to any transfers to China under the Agreement, the fact that the People's Republic of China is a nuclear-weapon state and that the safeguards of the International Atomic Energy Agency (IAEA) or their equivalent are not required by the Atomic Energy Act for agreements for cooperation with nuclear weapon states. These arrangements will be published in the Federal Register using the procedure applicable to subsequent arrangements under section 131(a) of the Atomic Energy Act.

(B) That the Government of the People's Republic of China has provided additional information concerning its nuclear nonproliferation policies and that, based on this and all other information available to the United States Government, the People's Republic of China is not in violation of paragraph (2) of section 129 of the Atomic Energy Act of 1954.

The United States Government has received additional information from the People's Republic of China concerning its nonproliferation policies since the enactment of Public Law 99-183 on December 16, 1985, most recently, China's May 1996 statement, its May 1997 State Council Notice on nuclear export policy and its September 1997 nuclear export control regulations (all of which are discussed in the enclosed unclassified report on China's nonproliferation policies and practices). On the basis of this and all other information available to the United States Government, I conclude that there is no legal bar to cooperation in this area, and, in particular, that paragraph (2) of section 129 of the Atomic Energy Act does not foreclose nuclear cooperation. The Government of the People's Republic of China has made substantial strides in joining the international nonproliferation regime, and in putting in place a comprehensive system of nuclear-related, nationwide export controls, since the nuclear cooperation agreement was concluded in 1985. I believe the initiation of cooperation under the Agreement will bring significant nonproliferation benefits to the United States.

(C) That the obligation to consider favorably a request to carry out activities described in Article 5(2) of the Agreement shall not prejudice the decision of the United States to approve or disapprove such a request.

The U.S. consent rights provided for in Article 5(2) of the Agreement satisfy this standard because the specific language used ensures that the United States must exercise an approval right before the activity in question is carried out. During Congressional consideration of the Agreement, the executive branch provided both the Senate Foreign Relations Committee and the House Foreign Affairs Committee with a legal memorandum on issues relating to the Agreement which covered this point in detail.

In accordance with Public Law 101-246, I have certified that China has provided clear and unequivocal assurances to the United States that it is not assisting and will not assist any nonnuclear-weapon state, either directly or indirectly, in acquiring nuclear explosive devices or the material and components for such devices. This certification is based on the statements, policies, and actions by China that were discussed above in connection with the certification under section (b)(1)(A) of Public Law 99-183.

Pursuant to the authority vested in me by section 902(b)(2) of the Foreign Relations Authorization Act, Fiscal Years 1990 and 1991 (Public Law 101-246), I hereby report to the Congress that it is in the national interest of the United States to terminate the suspensions and automatic disapprovals under section 902(a)(6). A document discussing the rationale for this report is enclosed. I believe the Agreement will have a significant, positive impact in promoting U.S. nonproliferation and national security interests with China and in building a stronger bilateral relationship with China based on respect for international norms.

This report under section 902(b)(2) satisfies the condition under section 902(a)(6)(B)(iii).

With the submission of the certifications and reports called for by Public Law 99-183 and Public Law 101-246, I am pleased that the process is underway to begin nuclear cooperation with China.

Sincerely,

William J. Clinton

The Honorable Benjamin A. Gilman
Chairman
Committee on International Relations
House of Representatives
Washington, D.C. 20515

Enclosures:
1. Presidential Determination
2. Unclassified Report on China's Nonproliferation Policies, Practices and Assurances Required by Public Law 99-103
3. U.S.-PRC Memorandum of Understanding on Exchanges of Information and Visits and Side Notes on Protection of Business Confidential Information
4. Basis for certification under section (b)(1)(A) of Public Law 99-183
5. Rationale for Report Required by Public Law 101-246

THE WHITE HOUSE

WASHINGTON

January 12, 1998

Presidential Determination
No. 98-10

MEMORANDUM FOR THE SECRETARY OF STATE

SUBJECT: Certification Pursuant to Section (b)(1) of Public Law 99-183 and to Section 902(a)(6)(B) of Public Law 101-246

Pursuant to section (b)(1) of Public Law 99-183 of December 16, 1985, relating to the approval and implementation of the Agreement for Cooperation Between the United States and the People's Republic of China, I hereby certify that:

(A) the reciprocal arrangements made pursuant to Article 8 of the Agreement have been designed to be effective in ensuring that any nuclear material, facilities, or components provided under the Agreement shall be utilized solely for intended peaceful purposes as set forth in the Agreement;

(B) the Government of the People's Republic of China has provided additional information concerning its nuclear non-proliferation policies and that, based on this and all other information available to the United States Government, the People's Republic of China is not in violation of paragraph (2) of section 129 of the Atomic Energy Act of 1954; and

(C) the obligation to consider favorably a request to carry out activities described in Article 5(2) of the Agreement shall not prejudice the decision of the United States to approve or disapprove such a request.

Pursuant to section 902(a)(6)(B)(i) of Public Law 101-246, I hereby certify that the People's Republic of China has provided clear and unequivocal assurances to the United States that it is not assisting and will not assist any nonnuclear-weapon state, either directly or indirectly, in acquiring nuclear explosive devices or the material and components for such devices.

You are authorized and directed to publish this determination in the Federal Register.

William J. Clinton

Unclassified Report to Congress on the Nonproliferation Policies and Practices of the People's Republic of China

Summary

China's policy toward the proliferation of nuclear weapons has undergone major and positive changes since the early 1980s. For more than three decades after World War II, China not only remained aloof from international nuclear affairs but also adopted an attitude openly critical of the Treaty on the Non-Proliferation of Nuclear Weapons (NPT). China did not require safeguards on its nuclear exports to non-nuclear weapon states and did not establish effective nuclear export controls of the type adopted by members in good standing of the international nonproliferation community. Most significantly, China provided assistance to Pakistan's unsafeguarded nuclear program.

Beginning in the early 1980s, however, China began emerging from its isolation. It became a member of the International Atomic Energy Agency (IAEA) in 1984, adopted a policy of requiring IAEA safeguards on its nuclear exports, announced that it would not assist other countries to develop nuclear weapons, and in 1989 concluded an agreement with the IAEA for the application of safeguards in China. In 1992, China set aside its criticism of the NPT and became a party to the Treaty, thereby assuming legally binding commitments not to assist non-nuclear weapon states to acquire or manufacture nuclear weapons and to require safeguards on its nuclear exports to non-nuclear weapon states. In 1995, China supported the indefinite extension of the NPT. In 1996, China announced a moratorium on nuclear explosive testing in July and signed the Comprehensive Test Ban Treaty (CTBT) in September. Also in 1996, China publicly committed itself not to assist unsafeguarded nuclear facilities.

With respect to nuclear export controls, China took a number of steps in 1997 to establish an effective and comprehensive national nuclear export control system. In May 1997, China's State Council approved a circular notice to government and industry requiring strict implementation of China's nuclear export policy of not assisting other countries to acquire nuclear weapons. This notice was supplemented in June by China's publication of a list of controlled nuclear dual-use items identical to the list adopted by the Nuclear Suppliers Group. Also in May, China attended the Zangger Committee's semiannual meeting as an observer, and in October China attended the Zangger Committee as a full member. In September 1997, China promulgated nation-wide nuclear export control regulations accompanied by a list of controlled nuclear items which the Chinese side stated is identical to the trigger list adopted by the Nuclear Suppliers Group. The new nuclear export control regulations restate China's nuclear export policy that: 1) all exports are for peaceful purposes only; 2) recipients must accept IAEA safeguards; and 3) no reexport to a third country without Chinese government approval. China is finalizing a similar system of export controls on nuclear-related, dual-use items. China has also stated that government departments have the right to exercise "catch-all" authority over nuclear-related dual-use items. China confirmed publicly in October 1997 that its regulations strictly prohibit any exchange of nuclear weapons-related technology with other countries and provide for a denial of assistance to nuclear explosive activities in addition to unsafeguarded nuclear facilities (attached).

China's nuclear cooperation with Iran has significantly lessened over the past two years. The sale of a uranium conversion facility, regarded as a key link in Iran's nuclear weapons program, has been suspended, and such minimal cooperation as is presently ongoing does not present a proliferation threat and will be completed in a relatively short time. China has provided a clear assurance that it is not going to engage in new nuclear cooperation with Iran.

China appears to be acting consistently with its May 1996 commitment not to provide assistance to unsafeguarded nuclear facilities. We are not aware of any transfers of equipment or material by Chinese entities to Pakistan's unsafeguarded nuclear program. We have discussed with Chinese officials the need for a clear understanding of what this commitment entails and are confident that we share a mutual understanding on this issue, including the prohibition on any transfer of nuclear weapons-related technology or information to non-nuclear weapons states. While we have discussed with Chinese officials specified cases of potential concern involving contacts between Chinese entities and elements associated with Pakistan's nuclear weapons program, our current information indicates that China appears to be acting consistently with its May 1996 statement. We will continue to monitor China's nuclear export and nonproliferation policies and practices carefully.

This report discusses the evolution of Chinese nonproliferation policies and practices and assurances and describes the assurances provided by China on nonproliferation and nuclear cooperation matters.

Pre-1983 Approach to Nonproliferation and Nuclear Trade

Throughout the era of Mao Zedong, the People's Republic of China (PRC) generally remained aloof from the international community on nuclear matters. Domestically, it focused almost completely on its military nuclear program. Some limited civil nuclear research was conducted as an offshoot of the military nuclear effort, but the PRC had no serious civil nuclear energy or research program. Internationally, the PRC had little or no involvement with other countries or international organizations in the peaceful uses of nuclear energy. It did not belong to the International Atomic Energy Agency (IAEA). It did not become a party to the Treaty on the Non-Proliferation of Nuclear Weapons (NPT) or associate itself with the principles of the NPT.

During the 1960s and 1970s, China's position on nuclear proliferation was closely tied with its position on superpower disarmament and its aspirations for leadership of the Third World. China argued that the spread of nuclear weapons to additional countries would diminish the power of the United States and the Soviet Union, and rejected the view that an increase in the number of nuclear-weapon states would enhance the risk of nuclear war. China also postulated that the introduction of nuclear weapons to nations in the Third World could increase the opportunity for revolutionary change that would work to the benefit of the Third World.

With the rise of the post-Mao leadership, increased emphasis was placed on economic modernization. The foreign exchange cost of modernization was seen to be great, and in 1979 Premier Hua Guofeng issued a directive to the Chinese government to increase China's foreign exchange earnings. The proposed expansion of economic activity also required increased energy supplies. To meet part of the projected increase in future energy requirements, China launched an ambitious civil nuclear power program. Because China had not developed its own technology for nuclear power generation, it decided both to import nuclear power plant equipment and technology and to develop its own industrial capabilities in nuclear power so that eventually it would be able to become self-sufficient in this area. To acquire this technology, China began negotiating with Western supplier governments.

With respect to Chinese nuclear exports, at the outset there appeared to be no central government involvement in overseeing and approving such exports. Negotiation of sales contracts was left to individual Chinese government export companies with responsibilities for specific materials, for which it was believed there were potential foreign markets. Most Chinese transactions in this period were arranged on a company-to-company basis with commercial intermediaries negotiating with the Chinese on behalf of a prospective foreign purchaser. Conditions for the export of nuclear materials at this time were generally minimal or non-existent.

Evolution of PRC Nonproliferation Policy During the Period of U.S.-PRC Negotiations on the 1985 Nuclear Cooperation Agreement

By 1982 some changes in China's approach to nuclear exports could be discerned. This may have resulted from a series of demarches made to China on its nuclear export practices by the United States and by several West European governments.

At the beginning of the Reagan Administration, the People's Republic of China expressed interest in acquiring U.S. nuclear power technology. The United States believed that discussion with the PRC on the terms for acquisition of U.S. civil nuclear technology would provide the United States with an opportunity to begin a dialogue on nonproliferation issues with the People's Republic. Preliminary discussions were held in Beijing in the fall of 1981 on the provisions of a possible U.S.-PRC nuclear cooperation agreement. Because of continuing U.S. concerns about China's nuclear nonproliferation policies and its relationship with Pakistan, Secretary Shultz raised the question of China's nonproliferation policy in Beijing in February 1982, and the United States invited the Chinese government to send a team to the United States to discuss nonproliferation policy and nuclear cooperation issues in detail.

The People's Republic of China accepted the U.S. invitation, and five rounds of negotiations were held between July 1983 and April 1984. In the course of these negotiations, the text of a proposed U.S.-PRC Agreement for Cooperation in the Peaceful Uses of Nuclear Energy was developed. Throughout these discussions, there was a continuing dialogue on the subject of nonproliferation policy. The U.S. side made clear to the Chinese in every round of negotiations that shared nonproliferation principles were an essential ingredient for bringing into force an agreement for cooperation as well as for the continuation of cooperation thereafter.

In mid-1983, during the early stages of our negotiations on the text of an agreement, the Chinese informed the United States that China would join the International Atomic Energy Agency (IAEA) (which it did on January 1, 1984) and that upon its joining, the People's Republic of China would require IAEA safeguards for its nuclear exports to non-nuclear weapon states. In September 1984, at the first IAEA General Conference attended by China as an IAEA member, the PRC representative announced the PRC's policy on safeguards:

> "China will, in exporting its nuclear materials and equipment, request the recipient countries to accept safeguards in line with the principles established by the

Agency's statute. In the same view, when importing nuclear material and equipment, China will also make sure that they are used for peaceful purposes."

The U.S.-PRC peaceful nuclear cooperation agreement was initialed during President Reagan's visit to China in April 1984. However, concerns persisted about continued assistance to unsafeguarded nuclear programs. Before forwarding the agreement to President Reagan, Executive Branch agencies felt it necessary to ensure that the United States and China had a full mutual understanding of our respective nonproliferation policies and practices. This was accomplished through additional consultations held with China. In these consultations, the United States and China discussed their respective policies on nuclear exports and assistance in detail. The Reagan Administration concluded in mid-1985 that a sufficient basis existed to proceed with the agreement.

The U.S.-PRC agreement for cooperation was signed on July 23, 1985, and transmitted to Congress the following day. Congress approved the agreement on December 16, 1985, but at the same time established a requirement for Presidential certifications and a report to Congress on China's nonproliferation policies and practices before the agreement could be implemented.

The Period Following Approval

The United States decided not to proceed with implementation of the 1985 nuclear cooperation agreement because of continuing questions about contacts between Chinese entities and elements associated with the Pakistani nuclear weapons program.

China's Growing Support for the Nonproliferation Regime: Adherence to the Treaty on the Non-Proliferation of Nuclear Weapons (NPT) and the CTBT

China's attitude toward IAEA safeguards and the NPT continued to evolve through the 1980s and into the 1990s. In 1989, China concluded a voluntary safeguards agreement with the IAEA for the application of IAEA safeguards in China. In 1990, China for the first time attended an NPT review conference and in early 1992 the People's Republic of China became party to the NPT.

During this period China also took further steps to strengthen the international nonproliferation regime. In November 1991, China informed the Director General of the IAEA that China would henceforth provide the IAEA information on its exports and imports of nuclear material. This commitment was made in the interest of assisting IAEA safeguards activities. The Chinese correspondence with the IAEA was published as INFCIRC 207/Add.2

in December 1991. In 1993, China joined the United States and others in supporting a UN General Assembly resolution calling for the conclusion of a nondiscriminatory, multilateral and verifiable treaty banning the production of fissile material for nuclear weapons or other nuclear explosive devices. At the 1995 NPT Review and Extension Conference, China supported the U.S. effort to extend the NPT indefinitely. China also played a positive role in support of the U.S.-DPRK Agreed Framework under which the DPRK agreed to freeze and dismantle its nuclear program. In 1996, China announced a moratorium on nuclear explosive testing in July and signed the Comprehensive Test Ban Treaty (CTBT) in September.

Relations with Pakistan Since China's Adherence to the NPT

Following China's accession to the NPT, the United States continued to be concerned about China's association with Pakistan's unsafeguarded nuclear facilities.

For example, in 1995 we received information involving nuclear cooperation between China and Pakistan, including shipment of ring magnets, a critical component of the upper suspension assembly of gas centrifuge machines. The ring magnet issue was raised on a number of occasions with China, including in discussions between Secretary of State Christopher and Vice Premier Qian Qichen in April 1996. In the course of these discussions, the United States received clarifications and assurances regarding China's policies toward nuclear nonproliferation and nuclear cooperation with other countries. The Chinese side assured the United States that China will not provide assistance to unsafeguarded nuclear facilities, including ring magnets, and that China stands for the strengthening of the international nuclear nonproliferation regime, including the strengthening of safeguards and export control measures. These assurances were reflected in the public statement issued by the Chinese Foreign Ministry on May 11, 1996 and were reiterated in the plenary statement delivered by the head of the Chinese delegation to the 40th Session of the IAEA General Conference in September of that year and reaffirmed during Secretary Christopher's visit to Beijing on November 20, 1996.

On the basis of a close review of all available information in this case, including the clarifications and assurances received from Chinese officials regarding past transfers and Chinese nuclear export control policies, the Secretary of State concluded in May 1996 that there was not a sufficient basis to invoke sanctions under the Export-Import Bank Act.

The publicity surrounding the ring magnet episode, and especially the widespread impression it created that the Chinese government did not have sufficient control over nuclear-related trade to ensure fulfillment of China's international commitments, seems to have had a significant impact on Chinese behavior. There has been a greater Chinese appreciation that "assistance" includes a broad range of activities, including personnel contacts, information exchanges, and transfers of items not specifically enumerated on control lists that could make material contributions to a nuclear weapons program.

Since China's May 1996 commitment, our information does not provide a basis to conclude that China has reneged on that pledge. China, however, is continuing to provide assistance to safeguarded facilities in Pakistan. For example, under a 1991 contract, China is building the 300 MW Chasma power reactor in Pakistan. We have not asked that China end safeguarded nuclear cooperation with Pakistan as a condition for implementing the peaceful nuclear cooperation agreement; but we have on numerous occasions warned China that the risk of providing assistance to the peaceful nuclear program of a country such as Pakistan (that does not have "full-scope safeguards") is that some of this assistance may be diverted to unsafeguarded activities.

During our discussions with the Chinese we have emphasized the importance of preventing diversions of equipment and information from Pakistan's safeguarded facilities to their unsafeguarded operations.

We have also stressed to China that its NPT obligations also prohibit assistance to nuclear explosive activities in Pakistan. In response Chinese officials have stressed the importance China attaches to controls on nuclear weapon-related technology and information and that such assistance to other countries is strictly prohibited. China has also declared publicly that its regulations prohibit assistance to activities related to nuclear explosive devices in addition to assistance to unsafeguarded nuclear facilities.

China's Nuclear Cooperation with Iran

Chinese nuclear cooperation with Iran had always presented a different concern than that raised by Chinese nuclear cooperation with Pakistan. Whereas China provided assistance over the years to Pakistan's unsafeguarded nuclear program, China's nuclear assistance to Iran has always, so far as we know, been limited to cooperation in the peaceful uses of nuclear energy and under IAEA safeguards. Nevertheless, because of long-standing U.S. concerns about Iran's intention to develop nuclear weapons, we believe that any nuclear assistance to Iran, whether or not subject to IAEA safeguards, would help to build an infrastructure that would be used by Iran to support nuclear weapons development. For this reason, we have urged China, as we have all other potential suppliers, to refrain from nuclear cooperation with Iran. This is a policy adopted by all other major nuclear suppliers except Russia and China.

Nuclear cooperation between China and Iran dates from June 1985, when a protocol for cooperation on the peaceful uses of nuclear energy was concluded during then-Iranian Deputy Prime Minister Rafsanjani's visit to Beijing. Cooperation reportedly was to include personnel training, and material and equipment supply. Under that agreement, Chinese nuclear entities undertook to provide cooperation to Iran on basic nuclear research and subsequently concluded contracts for the supply of several small, non-sensitive nuclear facilities. Chinese assistance to Iran has included cooperation on uranium geology and exploration, training for Iranian personnel, and supply of several small research reactors and related laboratory facilities. China has also provided Iran a small electromagnetic separation (EMIS) machine which is being used for stable isotope production.

The four small research reactors and related nuclear fuel are subject to IAEA safeguards and have been inspected regularly by the IAEA. The reactors are: two sub-critical assemblies, both use natural uranium fuel, one is moderated by light water, the other by graphite; a zero power reactor (ZPR) which uses natural uranium fuel and is moderated by heavy water; and a miniature neutron source reactor, which uses less than one kilogram of highly enriched uranium. None of these reactors pose any direct proliferation risk as they do not produce significant quantities of plutonium. The ZPR and the two sub-critical assemblies, however, could enable Iranian personnel to learn design principles that could have some, albeit marginal, utility in future efforts to design and construct indigenously a larger reactor for plutonium production.

In 1993, China agreed to sell Iran two light-water nuclear power reactors; but this reactor project was plagued by siting as well as other technical and financial difficulties. China has indicated that it will not implement this contract. China has also suspended the sale of a uranium conversion facility, which could have provided an essential element of Iran's nuclear weapons effort.

In discussions with the United States, China has made clear that it has decided not to proceed with the transfer of power reactors or the uranium conversion facility. It has also provided a clear assurance that it is not going to engage in new nuclear cooperation with Iran and that the last remaining nuclear cooperation projects will be completed in a relatively short period.

China's Policy on Nuclear and Dual-Use Export Controls

China has taken significant steps in 1997 to implement nuclear and nuclear-related dual-use export controls. On May 27, 1997, China issued a "State Council Notice Regarding Strict Implementation of China's Nuclear Export Policy." This notice stated China's policy of "not advocating, not encouraging, and not carrying out nuclear weapons proliferation, and not assisting other countries in developing nuclear weapons." In addition, the notice stated China's nuclear export policy that nuclear export items are to be used only for peaceful purposes, exported only under IAEA safeguards, and transferred to a third party only with China's permission. The notice highlighted China's policy not to provide assistance to any nuclear facility which does not accept IAEA safeguards.

The State Council Notice was sent to all Chinese government ministries and non-governmental entities, and directed that the export of nuclear materials, nuclear technology, and non-nuclear materials used in reactors would be exclusively undertaken by China National Nuclear Corporation (CNNC) and other Government-designated corporations. The notice provided for a system of peaceful-use guarantees, end-use certificates, and supervision by relevant government departments over all nuclear-related exports to both nuclear and non-nuclear facilities. The notice also specifically covered the transfer of nuclear technology, as well as the exchange of technical personnel or technical information.

The State Council Notice also provided that specific lists of items covered (including nuclear materials, nuclear facilities and relevant technologies, non-nuclear materials used in reactors, and nuclear-related dual-use equipment, material, and related technology) would be published by the Ministry of Foreign Affairs, the Ministry of Foreign Trade and Economic Cooperation, and the China Atomic Energy Authority. In our ongoing consultations on nuclear cooperation and export controls, the Chinese side stated that in June 1997 it had published a list of nuclear-related dual-use items and that this list is identical to the dual-use list created by the Nuclear Suppliers Group (NSG), as published in IAEA INFCIRC 254, Part 2.

While the State Council Notice was a significant step forward, the United States continued to urge China to promulgate detailed nuclear and dual-use export controls. On August 1, China announced that the State Council had approved in principle nuclear export control regulations, and these regulations were promulgated by China on September 10.

The new nuclear export control regulations restate China's nuclear export policy that: (1) all exports are for peaceful purposes only; (2) recipients must accept IAEA safeguards; and (3) no reexport to a third country without Chinese government approval. The regulations require assurances by the recipient on physical protection and reaffirm China's policy of prohibiting assistance to unsafeguarded nuclear facilities. The nuclear control list issued with the regulations was later described as identical to the trigger list created by the NSG, published in IAEA INFCIRC 254, Part 1. An export control licensing system has been established which provides for review of nuclear export control applications. License applications are reviewed by the China Atomic Energy Authority, the State Commission of Science, Technology and Industry for National Defense, the Ministry of Foreign Trade and Economic Cooperation and when appropriate the Ministry of Foreign Affairs. Civil and criminal penalties are included for violators of the regulation. The regulations also provide that if the government of the recipient country violates a guarantee made in accordance with these regulations or if there is a danger of proliferation, the relevant Chinese government departments may terminate the exports.

China has also publicly announced that it plans to promulgate a final set of regulations covering the export of nuclear-related dual-use items by mid-1998, and has stressed that the May 1997 State Council Notice established controls on such items in the interim.

Upon joining the Zangger Committee in October 1997 (see next section), China issued a comprehensive statement of its nuclear export policy (attached). That statement reaffirmed the policies noted above, but also made explicit for the first time other important nuclear export control principles. Among these principles were that Chinese regulations "strictly prohibit any exchange of nuclear weapons related technology and information with other countries" and that China denies assistance "not only to nuclear facilities not under safeguards, but also to all activities related to nuclear explosive devices." Importantly, the statement also made clear that Chinese government departments have the right to deny the export of items not found on control lists if they believe the export may possibly cause nuclear proliferation. Such a "catch-all" control is an important element in any comprehensive export control system.

Chinese Participation in International Export Control Regimes

China has historically resisted participation in international nonproliferation and export control regimes. Indeed, it was not until 1992 that China became a member of the NPT. However, in May of 1997, after significant U.S. discussion on the importance of participation in international export control regimes, China attended the NPT Exporters Committee meeting (also known as the Zangger Committee) as an observer. The Chinese attended the October 16 meeting as a full member.

Chinese membership in the Zangger Committee is particularly important because it is the first international export control organization that China has joined. Membership in the Zangger Committee will expose China to constructive interactions in a multilateral forum, familiarize China with international export control norms and practices, and continue to develop Chinese expertise in this area.

Status of China's Nonproliferation Policies and Practices Today

The Administration's goals during our consultations with China on nonproliferation and nuclear cooperation have been consistent with the goals of the 1985 and 1990 legislation establishing certification requirements for implementation of the 1985 agreement. These goals have been to (1) terminate Chinese assistance to Pakistan's unsafeguarded and nuclear explosive program, (2) curtail Chinese nuclear cooperation with Iran's safeguarded nuclear program, (3) establish an effective Chinese nuclear and dual-use export control system, and (4) encourage China to join multilateral export control efforts. Obtaining these objectives would significantly strengthen the international nuclear nonproliferation regime and would lay the basis for satisfying the statutory requirements for implementing the 1985 agreement.

With respect to satisfaction of these objectives (and the present status of Chinese policies and practices), China has taken the following steps:

-- China declared publicly on May 11, 1996, that it will not assist unsafeguarded nuclear facilities. We have no direct evidence that China has transferred equipment or material to Pakistan's unsafeguarded nuclear program since that time, and we have no basis for concluding that China is not honoring its pledge.

-- China's State Council has issued a public notice in May 1997 providing guidance to non-governmental entities and all ministries, commissions and other agencies under the State Council on China's nuclear export control policies. This notice states that China's policy is not to assist other countries in developing nuclear weapons, that Chinese nuclear exports are to be used only for peaceful purposes, under IAEA safeguards, (subject to retransfer controls) and may not be provided to an unsafeguarded nuclear facility. The notice covers nuclear technology, exchange of technical personnel and technical information, and dual-use items and technology.

-- China published detailed nuclear export control regulations in September 1997 which contain a list of controlled nuclear items that are identical to the trigger list of the Nuclear Suppliers Group. China's public notice of May 1997 references a list of controlled dual-use items that is identical to the list adopted by the Nuclear Suppliers Group. China has stated publicly that it will publish regulations covering the export of dual-use items by mid-1998, and that all government departments have the authority to exercise "catch-all" controls on nuclear-related dual-use items. China has declared that it strictly prohibits transfers of nuclear weapons-related technology and does not provide assistance to nuclear explosive activities in addition to unsafeguarded nuclear facilities.

-- China has effectively terminated its planned nuclear cooperation with Iran, including the provision of power reactors and a uranium conversion facility. China has provided a clear assurance that it is not going to engage in new nuclear cooperation with Iran and that the last remaining nuclear cooperation projects will be completed in a relatively short period.

-- China attended the May 1997 meeting of the Zangger Committee as an observer and attended the Zangger Committee at its October 16th meeting as a member.

In summary, we believe that each of the U.S. objectives set forth above has been met, and that China has provided "clear and unequivocal assurances" that it is not assisting and will not assist any non-nuclear weapon state, either directly or indirectly, in acquiring nuclear explosive devices or the materials and components for such devices. In our view, these assurances are consistent with the requirements of Public Laws 99-183 and 101-246. The U.S. Government intends to continue monitoring closely Chinese nuclear cooperation with third countries to ensure that China carries out its stated policy. We also believe that continued and regular nonproliferation consultations with the People's Republic of China will offer the best opportunity to ensure a continued common understanding in this area and, through these interactions, to exert increased U.S. influence over the future direction and implementation of PRC nonproliferation policy.

中华人民共和国常驻维也纳联合国和其他国际组织代表团

THE PERMANENT MISSION OF THE PEOPLE'S REPUBLIC OF CHINA
TO THE UNITED NATIONS AND OTHER INTERNATIONAL ORGANIZATIONS IN VIENNA

(Translation)

Statement by Ambassador Li Changhe Of the Chinese Permanent Mission in Vienna at the Meeting of the Zangger Committee

16 October 1997

Mr. Chairman,

I am very pleased to attend this meeting of the Zangger Committee to represent China as its full member for the first time. China supports the general goals of the Committee, appreciates the positive role the Committee has played in preventing nuclear proliferation, and stands ready to conduct regular consultations with other member countries of the Committee of issues of nuclear non-proliferation and export control with a view to making joint efforts to prevent proliferation of nuclear weapons.

Mr. Chairman,

The recently concluded 15th national Congress of the Communist Party of China has reiterated that economic development is the focus in the work of the whole Party and the whole nation, and emphasized that China's modernization drive requires a long-term peaceful international environment. Therefore, China will continue its pursuit of an independent foreign policy of peace, and work for maintaining regional and global peace, stability and prosperity . To prevent weapons of mass destruction of all descriptions, including nuclear weapons, is an important component of this foreign policy of peace.

As a member of the International Atomic Energy Agency and State Party to the Non-proliferation Treaty, China adheres to the policy that it does not advocate, encourage or engage in proliferation of nuclear weapons nor assist other countries in developing nuclear weapons. For many years the Chinese Government has exercised strict and effective control over nuclear and nuclear-related export, including exchanges of personnel and information, and has abided by the following three principles: 1) serving peaceful purposes only; 2) accepting IAEA safeguards; 3) forbidding transfer to any third country without China's consent. With regard to any nuclear export, the recipient government is always requested to provide to the Chinese side an assurance in writing to acknowledge the above three principles and the export can proceed only after approval by relevant Chinese authorities.

In actual implementation, China has always administered nuclear export and nuclear cooperation through a management which combines laws, regulations and administrative decrees. The State Council and the competent authorities of various industries have laid down strict and specific regulations on nuclear export and nuclear cooperation, and strictly prohibit any exchange of nuclear weapons related technology and information with other countries. Such management falls in line with China's national conditions and has proved effective in practice.

Mr. Chairman,

Along with the deepening of the reform and opening-up and the gradual development from the planned economy to a socialist market economy, the Chinese Government has in the recent period of time taken a series of positive measures on the basis of the existing management to further strengthen and improve the mechanism for nuclear export control. Our efforts in this regard are still going on. The following is my detailed introduction in this regard.

I. In May 1997, the State Council of China promulgated the Circular on Strict Implementation of China's Nuclear Export Policy, which provides that the nuclear materials, nuclear equipment and related technology, as well as non-nuclear materials for reactors, and nuclear-related dual-use equipment, materials and relevant technologies on China's export list must not be supplied to or used in nuclear facilities not under IAEA safeguards. No agency or company is allowed to conduct cooperation or exchange of personnel and technological data with nuclear facilities not under IAEA safeguards. I would like to point that the above regulations are applicable not only to nuclear facilities not under safeguards, but also to all activities related to nuclear explosive devices.

II. The Circular also provides that in conducting the above-mentioned trade or activities in nuclear facilities with a non-signatory to NPT, any Chinese agency or company should seek prior confirmation from the State Atomic Energy Authority whether or not the nuclear facilities in question are under IAEA safeguards and ask for in advance certificate of end-use from competent authorities of the recipient government and an assurance that the equipment so imported or cooperation so conducted will not be transferred to nuclear facilities not under safeguards. In case of no nuclear facilities are involved, competent authorities of the recipient government are required to provide in advance a reasonable and reliable end-use certificate for the equipment so imported and an assurance that the equipment so imported or cooperation so conducted will not be transferred to nuclear facilities not under safeguards. Such export or activities of cooperation can not proceed until confirmation and approval are granted by China's Ministry of Foreign Affairs, Ministry of Foreign Trade and Economic Cooperation (MOFTEC) and the State Atomic Energy Authority with regard to the above-mentioned certificates. Annexed to the Circular is the control list of dual-use items which is identical to Party II of INFCIRC 254. The promulgation of the above regulations has guaranteed China's effective control on nuclear-related dual-use items before the promulgation of relevant laws and regulations on the export control of such items.

III. The Circular has been formulated by China's State Council as empowered by the Constitution and is legally binding. All the departments concerned should comply with it and the supportive detailed rules for implementation will be formulated, no unit, companies or laboratories can be excepted.

IV. In order to transform relevant policies and regulation into law, China's State Council promulgated last September the Regulations on Nuclear Export Control, establishing in the form of law the three principles governing China's nuclear export and the policy not provide assistance to nuclear facilities not under safeguards.

1. The Regulations provide that nuclear export is monopolized by units designated by the State Council. No other or individual is allowed to engage in such export. A licensing system is applied to the nuclear export by the State, i.e. all the items and their technologies on the "Nuclear Export Control List" should apply for an export license. The control list is the same as Part I of the INFCIRC 254.

2. The Regulations provide that the State Atomic Energy Authority shall examine nuclear export applications. If the approved application involves nuclear materials, it shall be referred to the Commission of Science, Technology and Industry for National Defense for re-examination; if it involves other materials, it shall be referred to the MOFTEC for re-

examination. Any nuclear export which has a bearing on state security, social and public interests or foreign policy, the Ministry of Foreign Affairs should be consulted; when necessary, such export should be further reported to the State Council for approval. After approval, the MOFTEC will issue an export license.

3. The Regulations provide that if the recipient government should violate its commitment made under these Regulations, or if there is an imminent danger of nuclear proliferation, the department concerned of the Chinese Government has the right to suspend such export.

4. The Regulations provide that any violation of the Regulations is liable to punishment by law.

The Regulations are not only distributed and made known to all the relevant units through regular channels, but also published by the People's Daily which has the largest circulation in China and other newspapers and periodicals so as to ensure the broadest possible public awareness. On September 15, the spokesman of the Foreign Ministry of the Chinese Government made a special statement to comprehensively and authoritatively expound the policy of the Chinese Government on the issue of nuclear non-proliferation and nuclear export control in connection with the promulgation of the Regulations on Nuclear Export Control.

V. Relevant departments of China are stepping up their efforts to complete the export control regulations on the nuclear-related dual use items. The control list of the regulations will be the same as Part II of INFCIR 254 on dual use items. The export of all the items on the list will be subject of strict examination procedures. In addition, if the relevant department of the Government has reason to believe that the export of some item may possibly cause nuclear proliferation, even though the item may not be listed, the department concerned has the right to ban or suspend such an export. The regulations will be completed by mid-1998.

The promulgation and implementation of the above-mentioned regulations will basically systemize China's laws on nuclear export.

Mr. Chairman,

The prevention of nuclear proliferation is a long and arduous task which calls for the joint efforts of the international community. At the same time, the Chinese side wishes to emphasize that the prevention of nuclear proliferation should in no way affect or hinder the normal nuclear cooperation for peaceful uses among countries, let alone be used as an excuse for discrimination and even application of willful sanctions against developing countries. The prevention of nuclear proliferation and peaceful uses of nuclear energy constitute the two sides of one coin. The two promote each other and neither can be dispensed with. This is the consistent policy of China. The Chinese Government is ready to make unremitting efforts with other countries for the common development of both nuclear non-proliferation and peaceful uses of nuclear energy.

Thank you, Mr. Chairman.

MEMORANDUM OF UNDERSTANDING

The Government of the United States of America and the Government of the People's Republic of China (the "parties"),

Desiring to implement the Agreement ror Cooperation Between the Government of the United States of America and the Government of the People's Republic of China Concerning Peaceful Uses of Nuclear Energy, signed July 23rd, 1985, and entered into force December 30th, 1985 (the "Agreement"), on the basis of mutual respect for sovereignty, non-interference in each other's internal affairs, equality and mutual benefit, and

Desiring to exchange experience, strengthen technical cooperation between the parties, ensure that the provisions of the Agreement are effectively carried out, and enhance a stable, reliable, and predictable nuclear cooperation relationship,

Have established the following arrangements:

1. Each party shall invite personnel designated by the other party to visit the material, facilities and components

subject to the Agreement, affording them the opportunity to observe and exchange views on, and share technical experience in, the utilization or operation of such items. Opportunities to visit shall be accorded annually to reactors including their auxiliary storage pools for the fuel. Such annual visits shall be arranged at the time of reactor fueling if it occurs. Opportunities to visit all other items shall not be less often than every two years. When either party identifies special circumstances, the parties shall consult, at the request of either party, for the purpose of making mutually acceptable arrangements for the addition or reduction of visits under such circumstances in order to ensure that the objectives of Article 8(2) are fulfilled.

2. When material, facilities or components are transferred pursuant to the Agreement, the recipient party shall confirm receipt to the supplier party through diplomatic channels within 30 days after the arrival of the material, facilities or components in the territory of the recipient party. At the request of either party, the parties shall exchange information on the material, facilities and components subject to the Agreement. Such information shall include the isotopic composition, physical form, and quantity of the material, and places where the material, facilities or components are used or

kept. It shall also include information on the operation of the facilities subject to the Agreement which in the case of a reactor shall cover thermal energy generated and loading. The parties shall seek to resolve any discrepancies through diplomatic channels. The information shall be treated as confidential.

The above arrangements fulfill the requirements of Article 8(2) of the Agreement for the types of peaceful nuclear activities pursuant to the Agreement that each party had planned as of the date of entry into force of the Agreement. These arrangements shall enter into force upon signature and shall remain in force so long as the provisions of Article 8(2) continue in effect. Either party may request a revision of these arrangements, including the frequency, occasion or content of visits, at any time; any revision shall be made by mutual agreement.

Done at this day of , 1987

in the English and Chinese languages, both equally authentic.

FOR THE GOVERNMENT
OF THE UNITED STATES
OF AMERICA:

FOR THE GOVERNMENT
OF THE PEOPLE'S REPUBLIC
OF CHINA:

October 22, 1997

Dear Sir:

I refer to our discussions on the Memorandum of Understanding on visits and exchanges of information, as initialed on June 23, 1987.

In connection with these discussions, our Governments have reached the following understanding: In the event that access to commercial, industrial, or business confidential information is required in connection with the activities conducted under the Memorandum of Understanding, our two Governments will hold timely consultations, at the request of either Government and prior to such access being granted, to establish appropriate measures with regard to the protection of such information.

I would be grateful if you would confirm that this understanding is shared by your Government.

Sincerely,

Robert J. Einhorn

Robert J. Einhorn
Deputy Assistant Secretary of State

亲爱的先生：

你今日的来信收悉，该信全文如下：

“我提及我们关于一九八七年六月二十三日草签的信息交流和人员互访问题谅解备忘录的讨论。

“基于上述讨论，我们两国政府已达成以下谅解：如果为进行该谅解备忘录所规定的活动而需要接触商业、工业或企业秘密，应双方任何一方政府的要求，在同意接触上述信息以前，我们两国政府将及时磋商确定对上述信息的适当保护措施。

“如蒙确认贵国政府同意上述谅解，我将不胜感谢。”

我很高兴确认我国政府同意你来信所述谅解。

诚挚地

中华人民共和国
外交部军控司副司长 何亚非
一九九七年十月二十二日

Basis for Certification under Section (b) (1) (a) of Public Law 99-183

Introduction

The Agreement for Cooperation Between the Government of the United States and the People's Republic of China Concerning Peaceful Uses of Nuclear Energy (the "Agreement") was entered into by the United States in accordance with all the substantive and procedural requirements of the Atomic Energy Act, as amended, and the Nuclear Non-Proliferation Act of 1978 (NNPA). The Agreement provides, inter alia, that "material, facilities or components transferred pursuant to this agreement and material used in or produced through the use of any material, facility or components so transferred shall not be used for any nuclear explosive device, for research specifically on or development of any nuclear device, or for any military purpose" (Article 5). Recognizing that "this cooperation in the peaceful uses of nuclear energy is between nuclear-weapon states and bilateral safeguards are not required", the Agreement provides that "in order to ... ensure that the provisions of this agreement are effectively carried out ... the parties will use diplomatic channels to establish mutually acceptable arrangements for exchanges of information and visits to material, facilities and components subject to this agreement" (Article 8).

Senate Joint Resolution 238, approving the Agreement without change but requiring certain actions by the President prior to its implementation, was passed by the Congress on December 16, 1985, and became Public Law 99-183. Among other things, Section (b) (1) (A) requires the President to certify to Congress that "the reciprocal arrangements made pursuant to Article 8 of the Agreement have been designed to be effective in ensuring that any nuclear material, facilities, or components provided under the Agreement shall be utilized solely for intended peaceful purposes as set forth in the Agreement." In signing the Joint Resolution, the President noted that the arrangements to be certified were "called for by this article itself." 1/

1/ Weekly Compilation of Presidential Documents 1506-07 (Dec. 25, 1985)

A Memorandum of Understanding pursuant to Article 8 of the Agreement was initialed in Washington D.C., on June 23, 1987, by U.S. and PRC representatives concerning exchanges of information and visits to ensure that the provisions of the Agreement are effectively carried out. It covers all activities planned by either party under the Agreement.

In negotiating the mutually acceptable arrangements called for in Article 8 of the Agreement and the Joint Resolution, several factors were taken into account: 1) the nature of the cooperation that may take place under the Agreement; 2) the key U.S. activities essential to obtaining information, and confirming periodically through on-site visits, the exclusively peaceful use of any material, facilities and components in China subject to the Agreement; and 3) the fact that the PRC is a nuclear weapon state with an existing military nuclear material production complex.

Factors Affecting the Nature of the Arrangements Required to Meet the Standards of P.L. 99-183.

1. Nature of the Cooperation To Take Place Under the Agreement

The Agreement provides for cooperation between the United States and the People's Republic of China in nuclear materials facilities, components and technology for peaceful, non-explosive purposes. The only special nuclear material that may be transferred to the PRC in substantial quantities under the Agreement is low-enriched uranium, which is not directly usable for nuclear explosive or military purposes. No cooperation involving sensitive nuclear technology, sensitive nuclear facilities, or major critical components may take place under the agreement (without amendment). Therefore, the facilities, equipment and components that may be provided under the agreement are likely to be of only limited relevance to other than peaceful nuclear activities. Moreover, the U.S. export licensing process involves a detailed review of all proposed exports of facilities, equipment and components to ensure that such items will not provide substantial benefit to the PRC for military purposes including naval nuclear propulsion.

Any power-reactor-grade plutonium that would be contained in spent fuel subject to the Agreement is a far less desirable material for military nuclear activities than weapons-grade plutonium. Furthermore, no reprocessing of spent fuel subject to the Agreement, and hence, production of separated plutonium, may occur without prior U.S. consent and the development of additional, mutually agreeable arrangements for information exchange and visits.

2. Design Principles for the Arrangements

The arrangements made pursuant to Article 8 of the agreement are firmly grounded on longstanding principles of verification; namely that the verifying party must be 1) kept apprised of the status of the verified items, 2) able to confirm that status independently, and 3) able to do so for the life of the agreement. The Article 8 arrangements embody these principles and specifically include the following key elements:

1. The right to obtain the information required to maintain an inventory of all U.S.-supplied items, and of the material used in or produced through the use of such items;

2. The right to confirm periodically, on-site, the accuracy of the inventory and the specified peaceful use of all items on this inventory;

3. The right to obtain this information, and to conduct on-site confirmation of this information, for as long as any such inventory items remain in China or under its control.

These elements are similar to those in any verification system, including those administered by the International Atomic Energy Agency (IAEA). However, neither the Atomic Energy Act, the NNPA, the Agreement, nor the Joint Resolution requires IAEA safeguards. 2/ The Article 8 arrangements therefore are not to be evaluated as though China were a non-nuclear weapon state

2/ See Atomic Energy Act, sections 123 a(1), 127 (1) (requiring IAEA safeguards only on exports to non-nuclear weapon states) ; Report of the House Foreign Affairs Committee with Respect to the Agreement for Cooperation Between the United States and the People's Republic of China Concerning Peaceful Uses of Nuclear Energy, H. Rep 99-382, 99th Cong. 1st Sess. at 4 (IAEA safeguards not required); Cong. Rec. S1607-08 (Nov. 21, 1985) Statement by Senator Glenn that Joint Resolution does not require equivalent of IAEA safeguards.

subject to the IAEA system of verification, but rather in terms of the unique attributes of China and the type of cooperation authorized under the Agreement.

3. China as a Nuclear Weapon State

The PRC is a nuclear weapon state and has in place dedicated facilities to produce large quantities of highly enriched uranium and weapons-grade plutonium for its nuclear weapons program. Because the PRC already has a dedicated program to meet its military needs, its incentive to transfer material from civil to military nuclear activities is extremely low.

Moreover, there would be substantial costs associated with the exposure of an effort to utilize items subject to the agreement for other than their intended peaceful purposes. If the PRC were to use items subject to the U.S.-PRC Agreement for other than intended peaceful purposes as set forth in the Agreement, it would be taking several risks: nuclear relations with the United States would be disrupted; the overall bilateral relationship with the United States would be seriously damaged; the success of the PRC nuclear power program, which depends in large part on the involvement of Western nuclear suppliers, would be endangered; the PRC's credibility in the international nuclear field would be lost; and its ability to implement the PRC's own international nuclear cooperation policy, which requires peaceful use and other binding commitments from its cooperating partners, would be adversely affected.

Details of the Arrangements

The details of the arrangements agreed to by the PRC in the Memorandum of Understanding are discussed below within the framework of the key elements of the design. The arrangements provide the United States with full knowledge of what items are subject to the Agreement, how they are used, and where they are located. This information will be confirmed periodically through on-site visits. For reactors, which are likely to be the focal point of any cooperation under the agreement, the visits are to be timed to provide access to the reactor core as well as to spent-fuel ponds during reactor refueling.

The first key element is the United States right to obtain information for the U.S. inventory of all items subject to the Agreement. This is established in two parts of paragraph 2 of the

Memorandum of Understanding. The right to information required for placing on the inventory all items transferred to the PRC by the United States is provided for as follows:

-- "When material, facilities or components are transferred

pursuant to the Agreement, the recipient party shall confirm receipt to the supplier party through diplomatic channels within 30 days after the arrival of the material, facilities or components in the territory of the recipient party."

The right to information necessary for checking and updating that inventory in regard to both the items transferred and the material used in or produced through the use of such items is also provided for:

-- "At the request of either party, the parties shall exchange information on the material, facilities and components subject to the Agreement."

Through these provisions the United States is assured of the necessary technical information to permit a detailed accounting of where and how items are being used, which in turn forms the basis for meaningful visits to those items:

-- "Such information shall include the isotopic composition, physical form, and quantity of the material, and places where the material, facilities or components are used or kept. It shall include information on the operation of the facilities subject to the agreement which in the case of a reactor shall cover thermal energy generated and loading".

These provisions on the exchanges of information under the Article 8(2) arrangements are complemented by two provisions in the body of the Agreement, i.e., Article 8(1) and 8(3):

-- "The parties shall consult at the request of either party regarding the implementation of the agreement, the development of further cooperation in the field of peaceful uses of nuclear energy, and other matters of mutual concern".

-- "The parties shall exchange views and information on the establishment and operation of their respective national accounting and control systems for source and special nuclear material subject to this agreement."

Consultations on specific topics concerning cooperation under the Agreement are also provided for in Articles 5(2), 6(3), 7(1) and 9 of the Agreement.

The second key element of the Article 8(2) arrangements is the U.S. right to periodic on-site confirmation of inventory items and their use. This is established through four provisions of the arrangements. First, the basic right for U.S. visits and access to items is provided for in paragraph 1 of the Memorandum of Understanding:

-- "Each party shall invite personnel designated by the other party to visit the material, facilities and components subject to the Agreement, affording them the opportunity to observe and exchange views on, and share technical experience in, the utilization or operation of such items."

Second, paragraph 1 of the Memorandum of Understanding guarantees the United States the right to visit reactors in China that are on the U.S. inventory once each year; these visits, for maximum effectiveness, can be timed to coincide with reactor fueling, when it is possible to observe most advantageously the parts of an operational reactor:

-- "Opportunities to visit shall be accorded annually to reactors including their auxiliary storage pools for the fuel. Such annual visits shall be arranged at the time of reactor fueling if it occurs."

Third, the same paragraph of the Memorandum of Understanding guarantees that all items in China that are on the U.S. inventory may be visited by U.S. personnel at least every two years:

-- "Opportunities to visit all other items shall not be less often than every two years."

Fourth, also in that same paragraph of the Memorandum of Understanding, adjustments in the timing of visits may be made when special circumstances arise:

-- "When either party identifies special circumstances, the parties shall consult, at the request of either party, for the purpose of making mutually acceptable arrangements for the addition or reduction of visits under such circumstances in order to ensure that the objectives of Article 8(2) are fulfilled."

The third key element in the Article 8(2) arrangements concerns the duration of U.S. rights to obtain information required to maintain the U.S. inventory and periodically to confirm the accuracy of that information through on-site visits by U.S. personnel to China. Paragraph 3 of the Memorandum of Understanding ties the duration of these rights to the duration of the Article of the Agreement upon which they are based:

-- "These arrangements shall enter into force upon signature and shall remain in force so long as the provisions of Article 8(2) continue in effect."

Article 8 of the Agreement remains in force as long as any items subject to the Agreement remain in China or under its control:

-- "Notwithstanding the suspension, termination or expiration of this agreement or any cooperation hereunder for any reason, the provisions of articles 5, 6, 7, and 8 shall continue in effect so long as any material, facilities or components subject to these articles remain in the territory of the party concerned or any material, facility or component subject to these articles remain subject to that party's right to exercise jurisdiction or to direct disposition elsewhere."

Therefore, the arrangements established by the Memorandum of Understanding remain in effect so long as there are items which need to be verified.

Conclusion

Taking into account that: a) the cooperation that may take place under the Agreement is limited and nonsensitive; b) these arrangements cover only those types of activities planned as of the date of entry into force of the Agreement; c) the Memorandum of Understanding arrangements negotiated with the PRC fully satisfy commonly accepted verification principles; and d) as a nuclear weapon state, the PRC's incentives to misuse items subject to the agreement are extremely low and the disincentives in the form of adverse international consequences are very high, we have judged that these arrangements will be sufficient to deter PRC use of items subject to the Agreement for other than intended peaceful purposes and will give the United States the necessary confidence that such misuse will not occur.

Therefore, we believe that the arrangements contained in the Memorandum of Understanding initialed by the United States and PRC on June 23, 1987, meet the certification standard of P.L. 99-183 that these arrangements "have been designed to be effective in ensuring that any nuclear material, facilities or components provided under the Agreement shall be utilized solely for intended peaceful purposes."

Rationale for Report to Congress that it is in the National Interest to Suspend the Termination of Nuclear Cooperation with China

This paper discusses the rationale for the report, submitted pursuant to sections 902(a)(6)(B)(iii) and 902(b)(2) of P.L. 101-246, that it is in the national interest to terminate the suspensions and disapprovals of nuclear cooperation with the People's Republic of China under section 902(a)(6).

The prospect of implementing the U.S.-China agreement for nuclear cooperation has provided strong incentives for China to cooperate with the United States on nuclear nonproliferation. In the course of over two years of intensive bilateral discussions, we have seen major and positive changes in China's approach toward its nuclear nonproliferation obligations and responsibilities.

-- It committed in May 1996 not to provide assistance to unsafeguarded nuclear facilities. We have monitored that commitment closely and have no basis to conclude that China has acted inconsistently with its pledge.

-- It is phasing out its nuclear cooperation with Iran. It suspended the sale of two nuclear reactors, canceled the sale of a uranium conversion facility and turned down requests to provide other sensitive equipment and technology. Importantly, it will not engage in any new nuclear cooperation with Iran and will complete its few existing projects, which are not of proliferation concern, within a relatively short period.

-- It is well along toward putting in place a comprehensive, nationwide system of export controls on nuclear material, nuclear-related equipment and technology. A May 1997 State Council directive provided legally binding guidance to all Chinese governmental and non-governmental entities on the control of nuclear and nuclear-related dual-use exports. On September 10, 1997 the State Council promulgated nuclear export control regulations, and China has committed to promulgating its dual-use regulations by mid-1998. China is adopting control lists identical to the Nuclear Suppliers Group's nuclear trigger list and dual-use list.

-- China publicly affirmed in October 1997 that it strictly prohibits exchanges of nuclear weapons information with other countries, it prohibits assistance to nuclear explosive activities (in addition to unsafeguarded nuclear activities), and that government departments have the right to ban the export of non-listed, nuclear-related, dual-use items if such an export poses a proliferation risk, i.e., so-called "catch-all controls".

-- It has joined the Zangger Committee, the Non-Proliferation Treaty's Exporters Committee, and attended its first meeting as a member on October 16, 1997. The decision to join the Zangger Committee marks the first time that China has participated in a multilateral nonproliferation export control regime.

In addition to these steps, China's growing commitment to international nuclear nonproliferation norms has been demonstrated by its adherence to the Treaty on the Non-Proliferation of Nuclear Weapons (NPT) and support for its indefinite extension, its termination of nuclear testing and signature of the Comprehensive Test Ban Treaty, its support for a Fissile Material Cutoff Treaty and its support for the strengthened safeguards system of the International Atomic Energy Agency (IAEA).

It is in the U.S. national interest to consolidate and build on the progress China has made in the nonproliferation area, and implementation of the Agreement for Cooperation between the U.S. and the People's Republic of China concerning the Peaceful Uses of Nuclear Energy will establish a promising framework for doing so. The Agreement specifically provides for bilateral consultations concerning implementation of the Agreement and on other matters of mutual concern, which will give the United States continuing opportunities to engage China on such matters as export controls and China's policies and practices toward nuclear cooperation with other countries. With the agreement for cooperation as a necessary foundation, China has agreed to engage in government-to-government cooperation in nuclear materials control and accountancy, physical protection of nuclear materials and facilities, international nuclear safeguards, nuclear-reactor safety, development and implementation of systems for control of exports of nuclear materials and other areas of mutual interest in the peaceful uses of nuclear technology. Moreover, the many commercial and governmental interactions that will be stimulated by the Agreement will afford us a continuing basis to evaluate and influence China's nuclear cooperation and export policies.

It is also in the U.S. national interest to build stronger, mutually advantageous bilateral relations with China based on respect for international norms. Effective implementation of the Agreement -- especially given the importance and sensitivity of the subject matter -- will make a significant contribution to forging such a relationship as we enter the 21st century. The benefits that will accrue to both sides under the Agreement will demonstrate to China the value of working with us constructively to meet international standards and promote common goals, and will create a useful precedent for future bilateral engagement and problem-solving. An improved bilateral relationship will give us a more promising basis to advance a range of important U.S. objectives with China, including in the non-nuclear areas (e.g., chemical and missile) of nonproliferation policy.

The United States also has an economic national interest in implementing the Agreement for Cooperation in the Peaceful uses of Nuclear Energy. The Agreement will enable U.S. companies to compete for contracts in the world's fastest growing nuclear energy market. These potentially vast commercial opportunities will give a large boost to an important U.S. industry, improve the U.S. trade balance with China and create large numbers of highly-skilled jobs at home. Given the highly safe and environmentally sound character of advanced U.S. nuclear reactor designs, these opportunities would also serve U.S. international nuclear reactor safety and environmental goals.

CRS

Congressional Research Service • Library of Congress • Washington, D.C. 20540

Memorandum January 30, 1998

TO : House International Relations Committee
Attention: Walker Roberts

FROM : Shirley Kan (ext. 7-7606), Coordinator
Analyst in Foreign Affairs
Foreign Affairs and National Defense Division

SUBJECT : Analysis of President Clinton's Certifications to Implement the Nuclear Cooperation Agreement with China: Nonproliferation Policy and Practices

In response to your request, we have prepared comprehensive policy, legal, and technical analyses of the President's certifications submitted for implementation of the U.S.-China nuclear cooperation agreement. The analyses are to help the Committee prepare for a hearing scheduled for February 4, 1998. This memorandum covers China's policy and practices related to weapon proliferation issues. In separate memoranda, Jeanne Grimmett of the American Law Division, provides legal analysis as to whether requirements of the laws are met, and Carl Behrens, of the Environment and Natural Resources Division, considers issues pertaining to U.S. exports and China's nuclear fuel cycle. We do not argue either for or against certifications. If you have further questions, please call at 7-7606.

China's Policies and Practices on Nonproliferation[1]

Long Process to Certifications

President Ronald Reagan signed the agreement on July 23, 1985. Congress approved the agreement but required Presidential certifications and a report before the agreement can be implemented. Congress passed the joint resolution (P.L. 99-183) on December 16, 1985. Because of U.S. knowledge about Chinese assistance for Pakistan's nuclear weapon program, no President was able to submit the required certifications about China's nuclear nonproliferation policy until President Clinton's certification on January 12, 1998. In addition, after the Tiananmen Crackdown of June 1989, Congress passed legislation (P.L. 101-246)

[1] For more information on Chinese proliferation and the nuclear cooperation agreement, see: CRS Issue Brief 92056, Chinese Proliferation of Weapons of Mass Destruction: Current Policy Issues, updated regularly; and CRS Report 97-850F, China's Compliance with International Arms Control Agreements, updated January 16, 1998, by Shirley A. Kan.

imposing sanctions, including a suspension of applications for nuclear exports. A Presidential waiver of that sanction was also submitted.

Certification on "Sufficient Progress". Under P.L. 99-183, President Clinton has certified that:

> the Government of the People's Republic of China has provided additional information concerning its nuclear nonproliferation policies and that, based on this and all other information available to the United States Government, the People's Republic of China is not in violation of paragraph (2) of section 129 of the Atomic Energy Act of 1954.

Section 129(2)(B) of the Atomic Energy Act prohibits U.S. exports of nuclear materials and equipment or sensitive nuclear technology to a nation that is found by the President to have:

> assisted, encouraged, or induced any non-nuclear-weapon state to engage in activities involving source or special nuclear material and having direct significance for the manufacture or acquisition of nuclear explosive devices, and *has failed to take steps* which, in the President's judgment, represent *sufficient progress* toward terminating such assistance, encouragement, or inducement. (Emphasis added.)

This language is similar to that in Article I of the Nuclear Nonproliferation Treaty (NPT). Phrases subject to the Administration's broad interpretation of whether legal requirements are met include "failed to take steps" and "sufficient progress."

Additional Information. The Administration cites the following as additional information from China on its nuclear nonproliferation policy.

- May 11, 1996, statement that China will not provide assistance to unsafeguarded nuclear facilities;
- May 1997 notice from the State Council (China's highest-level governmental body, similar to the Cabinet) on China's nuclear export policy;
- September 1997 regulations on nuclear export controls.

The President reported that "China has made substantial strides in joining the international nonproliferation regime, and in putting in place a comprehensive system of nuclear-related, nationwide export controls."

What's Next? The agreement is now submitted for congressional review. Under provisions of P.L. 99-183, the agreement would be implemented after 30 days of continuous session of Congress after certifications — starting when Congress reconvened on January 27, 1998. Congress may pass legislation to delay, add conditions, prohibit implementation, or deny funds for implementation. In the first session of the 105th Congress, the House passed a bill (H.R. 2358) sponsored by Congressman Gilman that would extend the period of review to 120 days and provide for expedited review procedures. Implementation of the agreement would mean that U.S. firms may apply for export licenses and foreign firms may apply to re-export U.S. nuclear technology.

Issues for Congress

The central issue in consideration of implementing the agreement concerns China's nuclear nonproliferation policy and practices. The Administration argues that China's nuclear nonproliferation policies satisfy the legal requirements, as described in the President's "Unclassified Report to Congress on the Nonproliferation Policies and Practices of the People's Republic of China." Some in Congress and elsewhere are skeptical that China is committed in policy and practice to nuclear nonproliferation. Some add that even if China meets the legal requirements on *nuclear* nonproliferation, implementation of the agreement should be tied to China's comprehensive record on the proliferation of other weapons of mass destruction (*chemical* and *biological* weapons) as well as *missiles* that could deliver them.

The Clinton Administration contends that it has met each of the following four objectives which provide the basis for implementing the agreement according to legal requirements:

- terminate Chinese assistance to Pakistan's unsafeguarded and nuclear explosive program;
- curtail Chinese nuclear cooperation with Iran's safeguarded nuclear program;
- establish an effective Chinese nuclear and dual-use export control system;
- encourage China to join multilateral export control efforts.

These and other questions will be discussed in detail below.

Issue: Should the United States hold China to a higher standard of goals as the basis for "sufficient progress" toward ending nuclear weapon proliferation activities?

The Administration argues that the four goals that it set were the achievable goals in negotiations with China. Some in Congress argue that the Administration's timetable was limited by a desire to achieve an agreement by the U.S.-China summit of October 1997, at which President Clinton first announced his decision to issue the certifications. Others contend that China should be required to meet a stricter set of goals consistent with U.S. nuclear nonproliferation policy to represent "sufficient progress" under the law. For example, before nuclear cooperation starts, some say that China should require full-scope safeguards in its nuclear exports, especially to Pakistan. (Full-scope safeguards are intended to prevent diversions of nuclear technology and materials from safeguarded to unsafeguarded facilities, such as those in Pakistan, by requiring IAEA inspections of all other declared nuclear materials and facilities in addition to the facility importing the supplies.) Requiring full-scope safeguards is a standard that the United States has championed for years. China is the only major nuclear supplier to refuse to join the 35-nation Nuclear Suppliers Group (NSG), whose members require full-scope safeguards.

Some argue that the Administration is lowering U.S. nuclear nonproliferation standards to go ahead with nuclear cooperation while China continues nuclear cooperation with Pakistan — which refuses to sign the NPT and allow IAEA safeguards at all facilities — and while China continues to refuse to require full-scope safeguards or join the Nuclear Suppliers Group. Critics add that going ahead with the agreement constitutes a "pardon" for China's continuing assistance to Pakistan. Others, however, contend that if Washington is lowering its standard, it is worth doing so to curtail Chinese nuclear cooperation with Iran.

Issue: Has China terminated assistance to Pakistan's unsafeguarded as well as nuclear explosive program?

The President's report as well as previous press and government reports state that after the agreement was signed in 1985 and after China's accession to the NPT, China provided assistance to unsafeguarded nuclear facilities in Pakistan. The most recent, public case involved the transfer of ring magnets in 1994-1995. After China was embarrassed and the Administration decided not to impose sanctions, China issued its May 11, 1996 statement on not providing assistance to unsafeguarded nuclear facilities. Critics point out that statement merely reiterated China's policy and commitment to the NPT. China provides nuclear assistance to Pakistan, a country that refuses to sign the NPT and to allow IAEA safeguards at all nuclear facilities. For example, China is building a nuclear power reactor at Chashma, in Pakistan, which will have safeguards, and China is exporting heavy water to a safeguarded Kanupp reactor in Pakistan. The Clinton Administration maintains that China is honoring the pledge of May 1996 not to assist unsafeguarded facilities, a pledge specifically meant for Pakistan.

However, because China does not require full-scope safeguards, there is still the risk of diversions to unsafeguarded nuclear facilities. For example, there is concern that Pakistan may divert Chinese-origin heavy water from the safeguarded Kanupp reactor to an unsafeguarded reactor at Khushab that is intended to produce plutonium. Also, it remains to be seen whether China will apply in practice the broad definition of "assistance," to include technological and personnel exchanges, in nuclear export controls. Third, China did not explicitly prohibit assistance to nuclear explosive programs in its May 1996 statement, the May 1997 Notice, nor the September 1997 regulations. Perhaps at U.S. urging to fill in the gap, China made a specific reference to assistance to nuclear explosive programs in the form of a statement made by Ambassador Li Changhe on October 16, 1997, upon China's joining the Zangger Committee (a multilateral group that agrees on nuclear export controls to implement the NPT). According to Ambassador Li, the May 1997 Notice applies "not only to nuclear facilities not under safeguards, but also to all activities related to nuclear explosive devices." Fourth, U.S. intelligence recently has had concerns about China's various instances or types of assistance to Pakistan's nuclear facilities. The Director of Central Intelligence (DCI), in a June 1997 report for the last half of 1996, stated China was Pakistan's "principal supplier" specifically for its nuclear weapon program.[2] In August 1997, the Arms Control and Disarmament Agency reported that, for 1996, "questions remain about contacts between Chinese entities and elements associated with Pakistan's nuclear weapons program."[3] The President's report of January 12, 1998, also alluded to concerns, saying that "we have also stressed to China that its NPT obligations also prohibit assistance to nuclear explosive activities in Pakistan."

---

[2] Director of Central Intelligence. The Acquisition of Technology Relating to Weapons of Mass Destruction and Advanced Conventional Munitions: July-December 1996. June 1997.

[3] ACDA. Adherence to and Compliance with Arms Control Agreements (for December 1, 1995 to December 31, 1996). August 1997.

Issue: Has China curtailed nuclear cooperation with Iran's safeguarded nuclear program?

The President reported that "in discussions with the United States, China has made clear that it has decided not to proceed with the transfer of power reactors or the uranium conversion facility. It has also provided a clear assurance that it is not going to engage in new nuclear cooperation with Iran and that the last remaining nuclear cooperation projects will be completed in a relatively short period." The Administration argues that it required China to go beyond the requirements of international law in curtailing Chinese nuclear cooperation with Iran, since peaceful nuclear cooperation under safeguards is permitted under the NPT. U.S. policy has been premised on the belief that even if Chinese (or Russian) nuclear cooperation with Iran is legal, such assistance is harmful to peace and stability in the Middle East.

As the Administration says, China has "curtailed" its nuclear cooperation with Iran; the cooperation has not ended. China apparently suspended its sale of nuclear power reactors to Iran in 1995. In August 1997, Israeli Prime Minister Benjamin Netanyahu reported that Chinese Vice Premier Li Lanqing assured him that China canceled the plans to build the reactors. In addition, China apparently will not transfer a controversial uranium conversion facility, ostensibly because of Iran's inability to pay. (Such a facility would convert uranium ore into uranium hexaflouride gas, which is used in uranium enrichment processes.) The Administration was said to have requested cancellation of the deal on the uranium conversion facility as a condition for the Presidential certification. According to press reports and confirmed by the Administration, on the eve of a U.S.-China summit in October 1997, Chinese Foreign Minister Qian Qichen provided a secret letter to Secretary of State Madeleine Albright promising not to begin new nuclear cooperation specifically with Iran, after building a small nuclear research reactor and a factory to fabricate zirconium cladding to encase fuel rods in nuclear reactors. U.S. officials say the two projects are not of significant concern for nuclear proliferation.

However, the failure of President Jiang to give a public pledge while he was in Washington and the reliance on another secret assurance is reminiscent of the secret promise China gave to the Bush Administration in 1992 on the MTCR, which the Chinese later contravened. The Clinton Administration says that this latest confidential letter of October 1997 may be shown to Members of Congress, although it may not be made public. The President's report also concedes that small research reactors, even if they do not produce significant amounts of plutonium, "could enable Iranian personnel to learn design principles that could have some, albeit marginal, utility in future efforts to design and construct indigenously a larger reactor for plutonium production."

China's apparent retreat since 1995 in nuclear cooperation with Iran may have resulted from several factors, including: competition from Russia's sale of reactors, concerns of Israel (a key supplier to China's military), a desire to improve U.S.-China relations, Iran's financial problems, and increasing recognition that stability in the Mideast helps to keep oil prices low, which contributes to China's economic growth.

Issue: Has China established an effective nuclear and dual-use export control system?

The Administration has pressed China to establish a comprehensive, nationwide nuclear export control system. A "comprehensive," "nationwide" system would mean legally-binding authorities that are implemented and enforced to control the export of nuclear as well as dual-use nuclear items and all types of "assistance" to include personnel exchanges, as well as cover the military and defense industrial sectors. China has issued a circular (or notice) and a set of regulations on nuclear trade, but no new export control laws. It is unclear whether a circular has the authority of a law in China; the Chinese have claimed that it is legally-binding.

On May 27, 1997, China issued "A Circular of the State Council Regarding Strict Implementation of China's Nuclear Export Policy." On the positive side, the circular was issued by the State Council (the highest governmental body) as a notice which reiterated China's policy on nuclear exports to local governments, ministries, commissions, and agencies under the State Council. The circular specifically mentioned "dual-use" facilities, materials, and technology. It also specifically covered professional scientific and technical personnel and technological exchanges. In addition to the Ministry of Foreign Trade and Economic Cooperation (MOFTEC) and the China Atomic Energy Authority, the Ministry of Foreign Affairs (which represents China on nonproliferation) has a role in carrying out the policy specified in the circular. However, the circular has not been published and does not represent a new set of regulations on dual-use nuclear exports. At the October 1997 meeting of the Zangger Committee, the Chinese Ambassador said that the regulations will not be issued until mid-1998. The President reports that "the Chinese side stated" that it published a list of nuclear-related dual-use items in June 1997 and that the list is identical to the Nuclear Suppliers' Group's dual-use list, implying that the Administration has not actually seen the list.

At U.S. insistence, China also issued separate export control regulations on nuclear trade — but not dual-use nuclear items — signed by Premier Li Peng on September 10, 1997. At the summit last October, the White House hailed these as "strict national regulations." On the positive side, the regulations reiterate and implement China's official policy of nuclear nonproliferation. In addition, China's defense industrial sector and military are apparently covered, since the Commission of Science, Technology, and Industry for National Defense, or COSTIND, is one of the three agencies to carry out the regulations. Also, most likely at U.S. urging, the regulations contain detailed definitions of what would be considered to be "nuclear exports" and "assistance," — including, for example, personnel and technological exchanges. Last, the Chinese government widely publicized the regulations in the official "People's Daily" on September 16, 1997.

However, the regulations also have a number of short-comings. They do not require full-scope safeguards for the countries receiving nuclear exports, an important standard in the international nuclear nonproliferation regime which the United States has championed. The principles governing nuclear exports do not include a ban on assistance for programs on nuclear explosive devices. The China Atomic Energy Authority (CAEA), another implementing agency, is headed by Jiang Xinxiong, who is also president of the China National Nuclear Corporation (CNNC), which promotes nuclear exports. CAEA is the part of CNNC that serves an official governmental role and represents CNNC internationally. CAEA and CNNC are known to be in the same building. The third agency charged with implementation is the Ministry of Foreign Trade and Economic Cooperation (MOFTEC), which also has a competing mission in promoting exports. Meanwhile, the Ministry of Foreign Affairs, which negotiates with the Department of State, issues official Chinese assurances, and represents China on arms control and nonproliferation, does not have a routine role in the review and approval process. The Ministry of Foreign Affairs may be "consulted" if a pending nuclear export is considered to impact national security, public interests, or foreign policy. If there is danger of nuclear proliferation, only MOFTEC has the right to suspend exports. These regulations do not cover dual-use nuclear exports, and China has said that regulations for those will not be issued until at least mid-1998. The regulatory provisions have not been enacted into law. No penalties were specified for violations, although violations will constitute crimes under unspecified laws. Being new regulations, there is no track record for implementation and enforcement.

Issue: How are the new export controls more effective than those in the past?

Some question the effectiveness of the new circular and regulations given that China has had export control procedures in place that did not prevent nuclear exports to unsafeguarded facilities. In November 1995, China's State Council issued its first public defense white paper entitled, "China: Arms Control and Disarmament." The white paper stressed China's strict control over nuclear exports and its nuclear nonproliferation policy. The paper stated, "only specialized government-designated companies can handle nuclear exports and in each instance they must apply for approval from relevant governmental departments. All exports of nuclear materials and equipment will be subject to IAEA safeguards. China has never exported sensitive technologies such as those for uranium enrichment, reprocessing, and heavy water production." Some analysts question how the new regulations are more effective than nuclear export control procedures in place in the past which failed to control exports to unsafeguarded facilities.

Issue: How meaningful are China's new nuclear export control regulations, if the government does indeed lack effective control over its state-owned firms?

The Clinton Administration has concurred with the Chinese government's arguments that it was not responsible for the export of ring magnets to an unsafeguarded facility in Pakistan nor for exports to Iran's chemical weapon program by certain Chinese state-owned enterprises. Some in government question whether the Chinese government can indeed control its state-owned enterprises, especially defense-related ones. In trade cases, the U.S. Department of Commerce ruled (in February 1997, for example) that NORINCO, a Chinese defense industrial company involved in arms sales (not nuclear trade), is under control of the Beijing government and that subsidiaries of NORINCO remain under its control. If the Chinese government does indeed lack effective control over its state-owned companies, that poses the question of how meaningful are any new export control regulations.

Issue: How significant have been China's efforts to join multilateral export control efforts?

The President's report notes that China, on October 16, 1997, increased its participation in the international nuclear nonproliferation regime by joining the Zangger Committee (a group of nations which agree on export control guidelines to implement the Nuclear Nonproliferation Treaty). The President also said that this membership is "particularly important because it is the first international export control organization that China has joined." The Administration argues that such participation will expose China to "constructive interactions in a multilateral forum."

Nonetheless, China remains the only major nuclear supplier to refuse to join the 35-nation Nuclear Suppliers Group (NSG). China's membership in the NSG would be significant because of its common requirement for "full-scope safeguards." (Full-scope safeguards are intended to prevent diversions of nuclear technology and materials from safeguarded to unsafeguarded facilities, such as those in Pakistan, by requiring IAEA inspections of all other declared nuclear materials and facilities in addition to the facility importing the supplies.) China's refusal to join the NSG appears to reflect an important gap between China's commitment to nuclear nonproliferation and international norms. Some argue that the United States would be lowering its nuclear nonproliferation standard to begin nuclear cooperation with China when it has neither joined the NSG nor required full-scope safeguards. In addition, some worry that rather than being a constructive member of multilateral groups, China could obstruct progress toward stricter export control standards. For example, after President Bush decided in 1992 to sell Taiwan F-16 fighters, China suspended its participation in the Arms Control in the Middle East (ACME), or Permanent Five, talks. Those talks were begun after the Persian Gulf War to reach bans on nuclear bomb materials and ballistic missiles in the Middle East. After China's refusal to participate, those talks were never revived.

Issue: Should non-nuclear proliferation problems be considered?

As Congress reviews the President's certifications, some would question whether China's comprehensive proliferation record, in missile, chemical and biological weapons, as well as nuclear proliferation, should be considered. The Administration and others argue that adding non-nuclear proliferation criteria would be changing the rules in the middle of the game, thus damaging U.S. credibility in future negotiations. Moreover, the law does not require consideration of non-nuclear proliferation matters. Others argue that chemical and biological weapons and the missiles to deliver them are the more immediate dangers facing U.S. troops, friends, and allies. Richard Betts, in the January/February 1998 issue of *Foreign Affairs*, points out that "nuclear arms have great killing capacity but are hard to get; chemical weapons are easy to get but lack such killing capacity; biological agents have both qualities." Indeed, the Pentagon decided in December 1997 to vaccinate all military personnel against anthrax.

Press reports have suggested — and the Clinton Administration's public statements and sanctions have sometimes confirmed — that China has violated certain international norms, including the Missile Technology Control Regime (MTCR) and Biological Weapon Convention (BWC). Moreover, if China's confirmed assistance to Iran's chemical weapon program continues, questions of compliance with the Chemical Weapon Convention (CWC) will arise since it has entered into force. In general terms, the Director of Central Intelligence (DCI), in June 1997, submitted a required report to Congress stating that during July-December 1996, "China was the most significant supplier of WMD-related goods and technology to foreign countries."[4]

Concerning missile proliferation, numerous press and official reports and statements, including one by President Clinton, have strongly suggested that China transferred 300-km-range M-11 short-range ballistic missiles to Pakistan in violation of its commitment to the MTCR. China also appears to be aiding Pakistan in building a plant to manufacture M-11 missiles or copies of them. Now, there is additional concern that Pakistan is developing a medium-range ballistic missile called the Ghauri, as confirmed in November 1997 by Gordon

---

[4] Director of Central Intelligence. The Acquisition of Technology Relating to Weapons of Mass Destruction and Advanced Conventional Munitions: July - December 1996. June 1997.

Oehler, the recently departed director of the CIA's Nonproliferation Center. China may be providing assistance in that effort. As for aid to Iran's missile efforts, there is now concern about Chinese, North Korean, and Russian assistance to Iran in developing the Shahab 3 and Shahab 4 medium-range ballistic missiles.[5]

In an interview in January 1998, Robert Einhorn, Deputy Assistant Secretary of State for Nonproliferation, publicly gave assurances that China has not exported "complete ground-to-ground missiles" since its October 1994 pledge. However, he conceded that China continues to provide components and technology to both Pakistan and Iran to assist their production of missiles.[6]

While China may not have exported complete ballistic missiles covered by the MTCR — at least since October 1994, there has been a trend with China providing the various assistance necessary for Pakistan and Iran to establish indigenous missile programs. Some analysts are concerned this is a dangerous development that may lead to self-sufficiency in those efforts. In addition, Pakistan and Iran are reported to be working on longer range ballistic missiles, possibly with Chinese assistance.

As for chemical and biological weapon proliferation, the Administration has confirmed that Chinese state-owned enterprises provided supplies to Iran's chemical weapon program. On May 21, 1997, the Clinton Administration imposed sanctions on Chinese firms. As for biological weapon proliferation, Secretary of State Madeleine Albright wrote in January 1997 that "we have received reporting regarding transfers of dual-use items from Chinese entities to Iranian government entities which raise concern."

Issue: Could there be a significant downside to getting Chinese cooperation on nuclear nonproliferation but not on other proliferation problems?

Some question whether there are dangerous implications from not getting greater Chinese cooperation in all proliferation areas. For example, they believe China's ending nuclear cooperation with Iran could have implications for Iranian programs in missiles and other weapons of mass destruction. The Secretary of Defense reports that Iran places high priority on expanding its programs to acquire nuclear, chemical, and biological weapons as well as missiles.[7] If Iran is determined to have some weapons of mass destruction, some question whether it may now turn more resources to biological and chemical weapons. Beijing may see missile and chemical-related transfers to Tehran as more important sources of leverage over Washington, particularly on disputes over Taiwan.

---

[5] For greater detail, see CRS report 97-850F and Issue Brief 92056.

[6] Transcript: Robert Einhorn Interview on China/Non-Proliferation. USIA electronic journal, "U.S. Foreign Policy Agenda," January 7, 1998.

[7] Office of the Secretary of Defense. Proliferation: Threat and Response. November 1997.

NUCLEAR CONTROL
INSTITUTE

1000 CONNECTICUT AVE NW SUITE 804 WASHINGTON DC 20036 202•822•8444 FAX 202•452•0892
E-mail nci @access.digex.net Web http://www.nci.org/nci/

China's *Non*-Proliferation Words
vs.
China's Nuclear Proliferation Deeds*

Date	What China Said	What China Did
1981	'Like many other peace-loving countries, China does not advocate or encourage nuclear proliferation, and we are emphatically opposed to any production of nuclear weapons by racists and expansionists such as South Africa and Israel.' *Yu Peiwen, head of Chinese delegation to Conference on Disarmament in Geneva, Xinhua, 8/4/81.*	In 1981, China supplies South Africa (at that time not a member of the NPT and pursuing a nuclear weapons program) with 60 tons of unsafeguarded enriched uranium. This enriched uranium may have enabled South Africa to triple weapons-grade uranium output at the Valindaba facility.[1] In 1981, other unsafeguarded Chinese exports include highly enriched uranium, uranium hexaflouride, and heavy water to Argentina, and heavy water to India. Both nations are non-NPT states with nuclear weapons programs at the time.[2]
1983	'China does not encourage or support nuclear proliferation.' *Vice Premier Li Peng, Xinhua, 10/18/83.*	In 1983, China contracts with Algeria, then a non-NPT state, to construct a large, unsafeguarded plutonium-production reactor. Construction of the reactor complex began after November 1984—well after China's April 1984 pledge to subject all future nuclear exports to IAEA safeguards, and while China is negotiating a nuclear cooperation agreement with the United States.[3] China also supplies Algeria with large hot cells, which can be used to handle highly radioactive spent fuel to separate plutonium.[4]
1984	'We are critical of the discriminatory treaty on the nonproliferation of nuclear weapons, but we do not advocate or encourage nuclear proliferation. We do not engage in nuclear proliferation ourselves, nor do we help other countries develop nuclear weapons.' *Premier Zhao Ziyang, White House state dinner on 1/10/84, Xinhua, 1/11/84 (Note: A US official later said that 'These were solemn assurances with in fact the force of law,' AP, 6/15/84).*	U.S. officials reveal that, in the early 1980s, China provided Pakistan with the design for a nuclear weapon, and probably enough highly enriched uranium (HEU) for one to two bombs.[5]

1985-86	"China has no intention, either at the present or in the future, to help non-nuclear countries develop nuclear weapons." *Li Peng, Chinese Vice Premier, Xinhua, January 18, 1985.* 'The Chinese made it clear to us that when they say they will not assist other countries to develop nuclear weapons, this also applies to all nuclear explosives . . . We are satisfied that the [nonproliferation] policies they have adopted are consistent with our own basic views.' *Ambassador Richard Kennedy, Department of State, Congressional testimony, 10/9/85.* 'Discussions with China that have taken place since the initialling of the proposed [nuclear] Agreement have contributed significantly to a shared understanding with China on what it means not to assist other countries to acquire nuclear explosives, and in facilitating China's steps to put all these new policies into place. Thus, ACDA believes that the statements of policy by senior Chinese officials, as clarified by these discussions, represent a clear commitment not to assist a non-nuclear-weapon state in the acquisition of nuclear explosives.' *ACDA, 'Nuclear Proliferation Assessment Statement,' submitted to Congress on 7/24/85 with the US/China Agreement for Cooperation, 7/19/85.* 'China is not a party to the NPT, but its stance on the question is clear-cut and above-board . . . it stands for nuclear disarmament and disapproves of nuclear proliferation . . . In recent years, the Chinese Government has more and more, time and again reiterated that China neither advocates nor encourages nuclear proliferation, and its cooperation with other countries in the nuclear field is only for peaceful purposes'. *Ambassador Ho Qian Jiadong, speech given at the Conference on Disarmament in Geneva, 6/27/85 (quoted by Amb. Richard Kennedy in congressional testimony, 7/31/85).*	In addition to covering up its export of the unsafeguarded reactor to Algeria, China secretly sells Pakistan tritium, an element used in the trigger of hydrogen bombs as well as to boost the yield of fission weapons.[6]

1987-89	'China does not advocate or encourage nuclear proliferation, nor does it help other countries develop nuclear weapons.' *Vice Foreign Minister Qian Qichen, Beijing Review, 3/30/87.* 'As everyone knows, China does not advocate nor encourage nuclear proliferation. China does not engage in developing or assisting other countries to develop nuclear weapons.' *Foreign Ministry spokesman, Beijing radio, 5/4/89.*	In 1989, China agrees to build a light-water reactor for Pakistan, begins assisting Iran's development of indigenous manufacturing capability for medium-range ballistic missiles, and assists Iraq in the manufacture of samarium-cobalt ring magnets for uranium-enrichment centrifuges.[7]
1990	"...the Chinese government has consistently supported and participated in the international community's efforts for preventing the proliferation of nuclear weapons." *Ambassador Hou Zhitong, Xinhua, 4/1/91.*	In September 1990, after Iraq's invasion of Kuwait and the imposition of an international trade embargo, China provides Iraq with lithium hydride, a chemical compound useful in both boosted-fission and thermonuclear (hydrogen) bombs, as well as in ballistic missile fuel.[8]
1991	'The report claiming that China provides medium-range missiles for Pakistan is absolutely groundless. China does not stand for, encourage, or engage itself in nuclear proliferation and does not aid other countries in developing nuclear weapons.' *Foreign ministry spokesman Wu Janmin, Zhongguo Ximwen She, 4/25/91.*	Sometime around 1991, China provides ballistic missile technology to Syria, including the nuclear-capable M-9 missile. In 1993, a Chinese corporation exports ammonium perchlorate, a missile fuel precursor, to the Iraqi government via a Jordanian purchasing agent.[9] In August 1993, the United States imposes sanctions on China for exporting nuclear-capable M-11 ballistic missiles to Pakistan.
1991	'China has struck no nuclear deals with Iran . . . This inference is preposterous.' *Chinese embassy official Chen Guoqing, rebutting a claim that China had sold nuclear technology to Iran, letter to Washington Post, 7/2/91.*	In 1991, China supplies Iran with a research reactor capable of producing plutonium[10] and a calutron, a technology that can be used to enrich uranium to weapons-grade.[11] (Calutrons enriched the uranium in the "Little Boy" bomb that destroyed Hiroshima, and were at the center of Saddam Hussein's effort to develop an Iraqi nuclear bomb.)
1994	'China does not engage in proliferation of weapons of mass destruction . . .' *Foreign Minister Qian Qichen, AP newswire, 10/4/94.*	China supplies a complete nuclear fusion research reactor facility to Iran, and provides technical assistance in making it operational.[12] China, with apparent U.S. acquiescence, agrees to replace France as supplier of low-enriched uranium fuel for India's U.S.-supplied Tarapur reactors. The U.S. cut off supply of LEU soon after India's nuclear explosion of 1974. This LEU supply makes it easier for India to concentrate other nuclear assets on its weapons program.[13]

1995	**'China has never transferred or sold any nuclear technology or equipment to Pakistan . . . We therefore hope the U.S. Government will not base its policy-making on hearsay.'** ***Foreign Ministry Deputy Secretary Shen Guofang, Hong Kong, AFP, 3/26/96 (after discovery of the ring magnet sale to Pakistan).***	**In 1995, China exports 5,000 ring magnets to Pakistan. Such magnets are integral components of high-speed gas centrifuges of the type used by Pakistan to enrich uranium to weapons-grade.[14]**
1996	**'. . . we have absolutely binding assurances from the Chinese, which we consider a commitment on their part not to export ring magnets or any other technologies to unsafeguarded facilities . . . The negotiating record is made up primarily of conversations, which were detailed and recorded, between US and Chinese officials.'** ***Under Secretary of State Peter Tarnoff, congressional testimony, 5/16/96.*** **'China's position on nuclear proliferation is very clear . . . It does not advocate, encourage, or engage in nuclear proliferation, nor does it assist other countries in developing nuclear weapons. It always undertakes its international legal obligations of preventing nuclear proliferation . . . China has always been cautious and responsible in handling its nuclear exports and exports of materials and facilities that might lead to nuclear proliferation.'** ***Statement by Foreign Ministry spokesman Cui Tiankai, Beijing, Xinhua, 9/15/97.***	**In July 1997, a CIA report concludes that, in the second half of 1996, "China was the single most important supplier of equipment and technology for weapons of mass destruction" worldwide.[15] The report also states that, for the period July to December 1996---i.e. after China's May 11, 1996 pledge to the United States not to provide assistance to unsafeguarded nuclear facilities—China was Pakistan's "primary source of nuclear-related equipment and technology..."[16]**
1997	**'The question of assurance does not exist. China and Iran currently do not have any nuclear cooperation . . . We do not sell nuclear weapons to any country or transfer related technology. This is our long-standing position, this policy is targeted at all countries.' Foreign Ministry spokesman Shen Guofang, Los Angles, 11/2/97, Reuters, 11/3/97.** **'I wish to emphasize once again China has never transferred nuclear weapons or relevant technology to other countries, including Iran . . . China has never done it in the past, we do not do it now, nor will be do it in the future.'** ***Foreign Ministry spokesman Shen Guofang, Kyodo, 10/21/97.***	**According to a CIA report, China is "a key supplier" of nuclear technology to Iran, exporting over $60 million worth annually. Fourteen Chinese nuclear experts are reportedly working at Iranian nuclear facilities.[17]**

End Notes

*** China's non-proliferation statements are documented in Rep. Benjamin Gilman, "China's Nuclear Nonproliferation Promises: 1981-1997," *Congressional Record*, November 5, 1997, p. H10073. China's proliferation deeds are documented in Steven Dolley, "China's Record of Proliferation Misbehavior," Nuclear Control Institute, September 29, 1997.**

1. Leonard Spector, *Nuclear Ambitions*, 1990, p. 274; Michael Brenner, "People's Republic of China," in *International Nuclear Trade and Nonproliferation*, Ed. William Potter, 1990, p. 253.

2. Judith Miller, "U.S. is Holding Up Peking Atom Talks," *New York Times*, September 19, 1982; Brenner, *ibid.*; Gary Milhollin and Gerard White, "A New China Syndrome: Beijing's Atomic Bazaar," *Washington Post*, May 12, 1991, p. C4.

3. Vipin Gupta, "Algeria's Nuclear Ambitions," *International Defense Review*, #4, 1992, pp. 329-330.

4. Mark Hibbs, "Move to Block China Certification Doesn't Concern Administration," *Nucleonics Week*, August 7, 1997, p. 11.

5. Leslie Gelb, "Pakistan Link Perils U.S.-China Nuclear Pact," *New York Times*, June 22, 1984, p. Al; Leonard Spector et al., *Tracking Nuclear Proliferation*, Carnegie Endowment for International Peace, 1995, p. 49.

6. Milhollin and White, "A New China Syndrome," *op cit.*, p. C4.

7. "Iraq and the Bomb," *MidEast Markets*, December 11, 1989, p. 130.

8. Tim Kelsey, "Chinese Arms Dealers Flaunt U.N. Embargo--China Ships Vital Nuclear Cargo to Iraq," *London Sunday Independent*, September 30, 1990, reprinted in *Congressional Record*, October 18, 1990, p. H10531.

9. *Export Control News*, December 30, 1994, p. 14.

10. Kenneth Timmerman, "Tehran's A-Bomb Program Shows Startling Progress," *Washington Times*, May 8, 1995. According to Timmerman, China and Iran did not report the 1991 purchase of this reactor to the IAEA.

11. Marie Colvin, "Secret Iranian Plans for a Nuclear Bomb," *Sunday Times (London)*, July 28, 1991; Russell Watson, "Merchants of Death," *Newsweek*, November 18, 1991, p. 38.

12. Gary Milhollin, Wisconsin Project, Testimony before the Senate Select Committee on Intelligence, September 18, 1997, p. 8

13. Mark Hibbs, "Reported VVER-1000 Sale to India Raises NSG Concern on Safeguards," *Nucleonics Week*, January 12, 1995, p. 1.

14. Tim Weiner, "Atom Arms Parts Sold to Pakistan by China, U.S. Says," *New York Times*, February 8, 1996, p. Al.

15. U.S. Central Intelligence Agency, Nonproliferation Center, "The Acquisition of Technology Relating to Weapons of Mass Destruction and Advanced Conventional Munitions," 1997, p. 5. See also Mark Hibbs, "DOD, ACDA Want China Accord Link to Other Weapons Export Limits," *Nucleonics Week*, August 21, 1997, p. 2; Tim Weiner, "China is Top Supplier to Nations Seeking Powerful, Banned Arms," *New York Times*, July 3, 1997, p. A10.

16. CIA report, "The Acquisition of Technology Relating to Weapons of Mass Destruction," *op cit.*, p. 5.

17. CIA report, *ibid.*; Con Coughlin, "U.S. Sounds Alarm Over Iran Nuclear Threat," *Sunday Telegraph (London)*, February 23, 1997, p. 24.

For more information on the U.S.-China nuclear agreement, visit the Nuclear Control Institute web site at http://www.nci.org/nci/nci-usc.htm

Sen Gilman

QUESTIONS

General

1. Why does the Administration want to implement this agreement? Whose interests are best served by proceeding at this time?

2. From a non-proliferation perspective, explain why implementation of this accord is a "win" or a "loss" for the U.S.

3. Do you believe that China has decided to become a responsible member of the international non-proliferation community? If so, what is your evidence for this?

- -- Let's explore this a little more. Would you agree with me that China's record of adhering to its non-proliferation pledges differs markedly depending on whether you are talking about nuclear or missiles or chemicals or even conventional weapons?

- -- How would you rate China's non-proliferation record on missiles? On chemicals? On conventional weapons?

- -- Should the Congress review just China's nuclear non-proliferation record as it considers this issue?

4. There are Members of Congress who are skeptical about any assurances we may receive from the Chinese to not proliferate nuclear materials, components, technology, etc. They would argue what is critical is China's record in adhering to such assurances and therefore, at most, the U.S. should only partially implement the 1985 agreement in order to judge China's record. Do you agree or disagree?

2. The US-China Nuclear Cooperation Agreement

1. From a nonproliferation standpoint, what benefits would accrue to the United States if the 1985 peaceful nuclear cooperation agreement is implemented?

2. How much value does China place on bringing into force the 1985 US-China nuclear cooperation agreement?

- -- How much leverage does this give us?

- -- Is this leverage usable mainly on nuclear-related issues? On other proliferation issues? On issues unrelated to proliferation?

- -- What are China's options for obtaining nuclear equipment and assistance elsewhere?

3. To what extent is China's nuclear power industry dependent upon outside suppliers?

- -- Where does China currently obtain its non-indigenous nuclear-related equipment?

4 .What is the nature and extent of cooperation between China and other nuclear suppliers?

5. How much cooperation do we receive from other nuclear suppliers in our efforts to moderate Chinese proliferation behavior?

6. We have not been notably successful in tracking the purposes to which US exports to China are put.

-- What commitments do we have from China that we will be able to verify the uses to which US goods exported under the 1985 nuclear agreement are put?

-- Given the frustrations of the past, why should we place much value on these assurances?

7. Why is China so much more responsive to US concerns about nuclear proliferation than about missile or chemical weapons proliferation?

8. Is there a proliferation risk inherent in the technologies or resulting nuclear fuel provided by the U.S. or other countries to China?

-- What are the risks of diversion internally to China's military nuclear infrastrucure?

-- What about the risk of China diverting to other countries' nuclear programs?

3. China and the Multilateral Nonproliferation Regime

1. As you well know, we did not succeed in requiring that China join the Nuclear Supplier Group (NSG) as a condition for implementing the 1985 law. Let me ask you a couple of questions in this regard:

-- Did the Administration formally ask China to join the NSG? Are there any reasons we would not want to have China as a member of the NSG?

-- Would you agree that, along with the Non-Proliferation Treaty (NPT) the NSG is one of the pillars of the international non-proliferation nuclear regime?

-- Isn't it a central non-proliferation objective of this Administration to bring nuclear supplier nations, such as China, in the NSG?

-- Once this agreement is implemented what will be the leverage of the Administration to get China to join and adhere to the tenets of the NSG?

-- Please give me examples of nuclear supplier countries with which we have implemented nuclear cooperation agreements that are not NSG members? (If the reply is Argentina or Brazil ask: Are you equating these countries proliferation record with China's?)

2. I understand that China became a member of the Zangger Group in October, 1997. Please explain to the Committee how Chinese membership in this group differs from the NSG.

-- Are you concerned that, given the fact that the Zangger Group is committed to applying full-scope safeguards within three years, that Chinese membership in that group will derail this objective?

-- Does membership in the Zangger Group obligate China to do anything it is not already obligated to do?

-- If not, is there any value to China's membership?

3. Why won't China join the Nuclear Suppliers Group?

-- What would the probable Chinese reaction be if the Congress insisted that China join the NSG as a precondition for certification under the 1985 nuclear agreement?

4. Is China a party to the Missile Technology Control Regime (MTCR)? If not, why not?

-- What pledges regarding the MTCR has China made?

-- What qualifications to these pledges has China made, and what is the practical effect of these qualifications?

-- Has China abided by the pledges it has made regarding the MTCR?

5. Does China possess an export control system that would be effective in detecting and blocking the export of items subject to MTCR restrictions?

-- If not, is there any reason to think China will create such a control system for MTCR items?

6. Has China ratified the Chemical Weapons Convention (CWC)?

-- Does China possess an export control system that would be effective in enforcing its obligations under the CWC?

-- If not, has China given any indication that it is serious about creating an effective export control system to fulfill its CWC obligations?

4. Chinese Export Controls

1. What is the status of China's implementation of nuclear export controls?

2. What is your understanding of the Administration's minimum expectation for what China has to accomplish? Should the August 1st decree, and subsequent September 11 announcement, by the Chinese State Council fulfill our expectations? If not, what more should be done?

3. What is China's record with regard to implementing an effective export control system to control chemical weapons and other weapons of mass destruction? Does their record in this area give you confidence that nuclear export controls will be effective?

4. Is China currently abiding by the provisions of the Australia Group?

5. Should we not insist on a minimum one-year waiting period for implementing the 1985 agreement during which China would prove to us that it has actually implemented an effective export control system?

6. Why does China still insist that no post-shipment verifications (PSVs) can be undertaken by U.S. Government officials to check on the end use of our dual use exports to China?

7. Maintaining a tight system of export controls requires three things: good laws, an effective regulatory mechanism to enforce the laws, and political will.

-- Please comment on each of these three things with respect to China's nuclear, missile, and chemical weapons exports.

-- How plausible is it that senior Chinese leaders would not be informed of potentially controversial Chinese nuclear, missile, or chemical weapons exports prior to the export occurring?

5. Chinese Nuclear Assistance to Iran

1. What is the nature and extent of current Chinese nuclear assistance to Iran?

-- Is Chinese nuclear assistance to Iran fully compliant with China's NPT obligations?

2. With respect to Chinese nuclear assistance to Iran that is compliant with China's NPT obligations:

-- Do we believe this assistance is being used by Iran to develop nuclear weapons?

-- Do the Chinese believe this? If not, what accounts for the difference of opinion we and the Chinese have on this issue?

3. Does China believe that Iran has a clandestine nuclear weapons program?

4. What would China's reaction be if Iran joined the ranks of the nuclear weapons states?

5. To what extent is Chinese nuclear assistance to Iran viewed in Beijing as a way to thumb China's nose at the United States?

6. Chinese Nuclear Assistance to Pakistan

1. With respect to China's May 11, 1996, pledge not to provide assistance to unsafeguarded facilities:

-- Has China lived up to this pledge with respect to Pakistan?

-- How certain are you that we could discover any activity that would violate this pledge?

-- Do we and China agree on the definition of the assistance that is prohibited?

2. Regarding the Administration's assessment regarding Chinese assistance to unsafeguarded facilities:

-- Do you believe that this assessment rest primarily on a failure to find evidence substantiating such assistance?

-- Or do you believe that we have positive evidence indicating an absence of such assistance?

3. What sort of assistance does China provide Pakistan's safeguarded facilities?

-- Is all of this assistance compliant with China's NPT obligations?

-- What steps has China taken to prevent unauthorized or illegal disclosures in interactions with Pakistani technicians ostensibly affiliated with safeguarded Pakistani facilities?

-- Do we think these steps are adequate?

7. Chinese Missile Transfers

1. Do you believe that China has transferred M- 11 missiles to Pakistan?

-- If so, did these transfers violate any Chinese pledges regarding the MTCR?

2. Aside from the transfer of complete M- I I s, what other missile-related assistance has China provided to Pakistan?

-- Does this assistance violate MTCR guidelines?

3. How close to completion is the Pakistani missile factory near Tarnawa?

-- How important was the Chinese role in the design and construction of this facility?

-- Does this factory have the potential of upsetting the present military balance in South Asia?

4. Has China sold complete missiles to Iran?

-- If so, which missiles, how many, and when?

-- Did these transfers violate MTCR guidelines?

-- What other missile-related assistance has China provided to Iran?

-- Did this assistance violate MTCR guidelines?

5. In its missile transactions with Iran, does China make a distinction between transfers permitted under the MTCR and transfers prohibited by MTCR guidelines?

-- Does the Administration accept these distinctions? Or do we have legitimate concerns about even those transfers that are not precluded under the MTCR?

6. Besides Pakistan and Iran, has China transferred complete missiles or missile-related equipment or technology to any other countries?

-- Which countries? What equipment or technology?

7. Are you aware of any instances where the Chinese government has intervened to block the transfer of missiles or missile-related materials, equipment, or technology?

8. China has argued that its missile sales to Iran are less provocative than U.S. F-16 sales to Taiwan.

-- How do you assess this argument?

9. Has there been any change during the past year or so in Chinese activities relating to missile proliferation?

-- If so, what is the nature, significance, and reason for this change?

8. Chinese Chemical Exports

1. In May 1997, the United States sanctioned five Chinese individuals and two Chinese firms for the "knowing" transfer of items that would materially contribute to Iran's chemical weapons (COO) program.

-- What was the nature of these transfers? Did senior Chinese of ficials know of or sanction these transfers?

-- Did these transfers violate China's CWC obligations?

-- If so, what does this say about China's commitment to the CWC?

-- What has been China's response to these May 1997 sanctions?

-- Has China acknowledged these transfers? If so, has China acknowledged the illegal nature of these transfers? Have we seen any changes in China's behavior as a result of these sanctions? If so, is it possible to generalize from this case that sanctions are an effective means for persuading China to abide by global nonproliferation norms?

2. Aside from the transfers that led to the May 1997 sanctions, what other transfers of CW materials, equipment, or technology to Iran has China been involved in?

3. What transfers of CW materials, equipment, or technology to Iraq has China been involved in?

-- to Libya?
-- to other countries?

4. Are you aware of any instances where the Chinese government has intervened to block transfers of CW materials, equipment, or technology?

5. Has there been any change during the past year or so in Chinese activities relating to CW proliferation?

-- If so, what is the nature, significance, and reason for this change?

Questions on China Nuclear Agreement

REP. HOWARD L. BERMAN
QUESTIONS FOR THE RECORD

•Has China ever provided the US with assurances that it would not cooperate with other countries in safeguarded uranium enrichment or nuclear reprocessing activities?

•How will China's joining the Zangger Group likely affect the ability of that group to reach consensus on the need for group members to require full-scope safeguards as a nuclear supply policy?

•Does China have any nuclear nonproliferation laws that require the imposition of a sanction against another country or foreign person that engages in any illicit nuclear weapons-related activity? Does China, for example, have any laws requiring sanctions against any non-nuclear-weapon state that detonates a nuclear device, imports or exports such a device or design information or components thereof, traffics in sensitive fuel cycle technology, or assists a terrorist group to acquire a nuclear device?

•The certification materials indicate a rather high level of US confidence that China will not resume delivery of a uranium conversion facility, will not deliver any power reactors, and will not engage in any other nuclear cooperation with Iran beyond the two ongoing projects -- would the US regard any subsequent Sino-Iranian nuclear cooperation beyond these projects as a violation of the terms for resuming US nuclear cooperation with China?

•Does China's pledge that it will not engage in any new nuclear cooperation with Iran extend to the delivery of nuclear dual-use goods? China has indicated that it will establish license requirements for dual-use goods on the Nuclear Suppliers Group trigger list -- has China ever given us any indication whatsoever that it will enforce a policy of denying applications for exports of nuclear dual-use goods destined for Iran?

•If the US resumes active nuclear cooperation with China while China continues to engage in nuclear cooperation with Iran, continues to deliver nuclear dual-use goods to Iran, and continues to engage in active nuclear cooperation with Pakistan without any requirement for full-scope safeguards, how will this cooperation affect US diplomatic efforts to discourage other countries from engaging in similar trade with both countries?

•China will reportedly continue to assist help Iran to build a facility to produce zirconium -- (a) Why does the Nuclear Suppliers Group include zirconium on its Trigger List? (b) What is the licensing status of such a commodity under US export controls -- why does the US control exports of zirconium? (c) How about production facilities and related technology for zirconium, are these too controlled by both the Nuclear Suppliers Group and US nuclear export controls, and if so, why? (d) What significance do you attach to recent press reports that China has been seeking a zirconium plant from South Africa? (e) If, as the certification materials claim, the US regards any nuclear cooperation whatsoever with Iran as contributing to Iran's nuclear infrastructure and thereby its reported bomb program, then what is the justification for the continuation of the two remaining nuclear projects in Iran? (f) How will the US acquiescence to continued Chinese nuclear assistance to Iran in these two areas affect ongoing and future US efforts to discourage other countries from continuing their own peaceful nuclear assistance to Iran? (g) Has the US ever issued a diplomatic demarche to discourage any country from helping Iran to acquire zirconium or its production technology or equipment?

•If China agrees not to negotiate any new nuclear cooperation with Iran, do we know now the full extent of China's commitments to Iran under previous agreements? Do we have specific texts of those agreements?

•China has historically engaged in far more dangerous nuclear cooperation with Pakistan than with Iran, yet the United States reportedly only insisted that China not commence new cooperation with Iran -- why did the US not insist upon a halt to all Chinese nuclear cooperation with Pakistan, given this unfortunate track record?

•Have any items (goods or technology) supplied by China to safeguarded programs in Pakistan ever been diverted to unsafeguarded programs?

•Will the US permit cooperation to continue if China: (a) Licenses and ships nuclear dual-use goods to Pakistan's safeguarded nuclear program? (b) Licenses and delivers nuclear dual-use goods to unsafeguarded facilities in Pakistan? (c) Assists Pakistan in the safeguarded production of enriched uranium or the separation of plutonium? (d) Assists Pakistan in the construction of a plutonium production reactor under safeguards? (e) Engages in future technical discussions or exchanges of personnel from nuclear weapons facilities in both countries? (f) Fails to take steps that are adequate to ensure against the diversion of Chinese nuclear items either from safeguarded to unsafeguarded programs in Pakistan, or via reexports from third countries?

•With respect to China's "catch-all" export licensing clause -- Does the regulation require licensing officials to deny licenses for the export of goods which an exporter knows or has reason to know will be used for a nuclear weapons-related purpose, whether or not the specific good or technology is on any control list?

•The DIA includes China's key nuclear groups -- the China National Nuclear Cooperation and the China Nuclear Energy Industry Corporation in an unclassified wall chart of China's "Defense-Industrial Trading Organizations" -- how are these entities tied to China's defense establishment?

--If US/China nuclear trade resumes, would these be the entities with which US nuclear companies would likely cooperate? What were the respective role of these enterprises in the ring magnet affair?

●Do we have clear and unequivoval assurances that China is not assisting and will not assist any non-nuclear weapon state, either directly or indirectly, in acquiring nuclear explosive devices or the material and components for such devices?

- Do we believe those assurances?

•Did the May 1996 commitment not to provide assistance to unsafeguarded facilities include technical assistance in our view?

•Have we verified that the June 1997 list of controlled nuclear items the Chinese have stated is identical to the Nuclear Suppliers Group trigger list but do we know that it is identical?
- Could you provide us with a copy of that list?

•The September 1997 list of controlled nuclear items the Chinese state is identical to the NSG trigger list but do we know it is identical?
- Could you provide us with that list?

•The Chinese stated in October 1997 that its regulations strictly prohibit any exchange of nuclear weapons related technology with other countries and provide for a denial of assistance to nuclear explosive activities.
- Have we seen a copy of those regulations?
- Could you provide us with a copy?

•Could you describe the nuclear export control system reportedly established by the Chinese on May 27, 1997, and how it works?

•How many times and when have senior Chinese officials assured us that they were abiding by their non-proliferation commitments?

•Have the Chinese provided the Director General of IAEA full and complete information on its exports and imports of nuclear material since its November 1991 commitment to do so?

•Does the US have the right to confirm through on-site visits the use of all items subject to the nuclear cooperation agreement?
- What assurances do we have that the Chinese will permit such visits take place in a timely fashion -- such as not been the case in regard to our MOU concerning customs inspections of Chinese prison labor products?

•Could you describe the assurances we have received from the Chinese concerning C-801(2) transfers to Iran?
- Is it our understanding that the Chinese will not transfer any similar type missile or production technology to Iran?

- When will such transfers cease?

United States Department of State

Washington, D.C. 20520

August 5, 1998

Dear Mr. Chairman:

Following the March 4, 1998 hearing at which the Honorable Robert Einhorn testified, additional questions were submitted for the record. Please find enclosed the responses to those questions.

If we can be of further assistance to you, please do not hesitate to contact us.

Sincerely,

Barbara Larkin

Barbara Larkin
Assistant Secretary
Legislative Affairs

Enclosure:
As stated.

The Honorable
Benjamin Gilman, Chairman,
Committee on International Relations,
House of Representatives.

QUESTIONS FOR THE RECORD SUBMITTED TO ROBERT EINHORN
HOUSE INTERNATIONAL RELATIONS COMMITTEE
MARCH 4, 1998

General

Q.1. How are US national interests served by engaging in nuclear cooperation with China and, in particular, how are our nonproliferation objectives fulfilled by such cooperation?

A. Nuclear cooperation with China serves US national interests in several respects. The United States will use the Agreement and its broad provisions for consultations as a framework to engage China on such matters as export controls and China's policies and practices toward nuclear cooperation with other countries. Implementation of the Agreement provides an effective means of encouraging China to live up to the nuclear nonproliferation commitments it has recently made. Proceeding with the Agreement will also put us in a stronger position to press for progress on non-nuclear nonproliferation issues, where serious problems remain in China's policies and practices.

We anticipate that implementation of the Peaceful Nuclear Cooperation Agreement will pave the way for useful cooperation with China on a range of important nuclear matters. One example is the conclusion of the government-to-government agreement anticipated in the October 1997 Agreement of Intent on Cooperation Concerning Peaceful Uses of Nuclear Technology. It provides for government-to-government cooperation in nuclear materials control and accountancy, physical protection of nuclear materials and facilities, international nuclear safeguards, nuclear reactor safety, development and implementation of nuclear export control systems, and other areas of mutual interest.

These and other interactions that will be stimulated by the Agreement will afford the US a continuing basis to evaluate and influence China's nuclear cooperation and nonproliferation policies.

We also expect commercial benefits from implementation of the Agreement. Although China is negotiating with a number of countries for assistance to its nuclear program, it clearly regards the safety, design, and performance of US nuclear equipment and technology very highly. Implementation of the US-China Agreement will allow US companies to participate in this major Chinese effort.

The benefit to US balance of trade with China and to US job creation is impossible to quantify at this early stage, but the market in China for power reactors alone is a multi-billion dollar one.

QUESTIONS FOR THE RECORD SUBMITTED TO ROBERT EINHORN
HOUSE INTERNATIONAL RELATIONS COMMITTEE
MARCH 4, 1998

General

Q.2. How much value does China place on bringing into force the 1985 US-China Nuclear Cooperation Agreement?

-- How much leverage does this give us?

-- Is this leverage usable mainly on nuclear-related issues? On issues unrelated to proliferation?

-- What are China's options for obtaining nuclear equipment and assistance elsewhere?

A. China clearly placed importance on implementation of the 1985 Agreement. China values highly the design, safety and performance of US reactor technology and has shown considerable interest in cooperating with the US in the nuclear field. Such considerations gave the Chinese incentives for meeting US proliferation-related concerns in the negotiations leading up to President Clinton's decision to certify China's nuclear nonproliferation credentials.

However, we should not overestimate the leverage provided by Chinese interest in nuclear cooperation with the United States. The United States does not enjoy a monopoly in the supply of nuclear materials, equipment or technology. Countries in Western Europe as well as Russia, Japan and elsewhere are fully capable of supplying nuclear technology to China. Indeed much of China's existing civilian nuclear program has been imported from other countries. China has purchased civilian nuclear reactors from France, Russia, and Canada.

Implementation of the 1985 Nuclear Cooperation Agreement will also put us in a stronger position to urge Chinese progress in missile, chemical and advanced conventional arms proliferation. Progress in these non-nuclear areas has lagged behind progress in the nuclear field. Implementation of the Agreement will demonstrate to the Chinese that if they take hard decisions and modify their behavior in an area of concern to us, this will open up mutually beneficial areas of cooperation. We want the Chinese to take similarly hard decisions in the non-nuclear area. However, linking implementation of the Agreement to further progress in these areas would not be effective. The Chinese would see this as moving the goalposts for nuclear certification, increasing the likelihood that they would look to non-US suppliers as cooperating partners.

QUESTIONS FOR THE RECORD SUBMITTED TO ROBERT EINHORN
HOUSE INTERNATIONAL RELATIONS COMMITTEE
MARCH 4, 1998

General

Q.3. Press reports as well as the Administration's statements have strongly suggested that even if China has curtailed nuclear proliferation activities, there are still significant problems in Chinese exports relating to missile and chemical weapon proliferation.

-- Mr. Einhorn you said in January 1998 that China is continuing to provide components and technology to both Pakistan and Iran to assist their production of missiles. Should not the leverage offered by the Nuclear Cooperation Agreement be capitalized on to further missile and chemical weapon nonproliferation, which many believe are the more immediate dangers facing US troops, friends, and allies?

A. We are concerned about China's missile export behavior. Chinese behavior in the non-nuclear areas, especially on missiles, has clearly lagged behind their behavior on nuclear nonproliferation issues. More progress is required, and we will be pursuing this vigorously with the Chinese in the period immediately ahead.

However, our laws related to certification require Chinese performance in nuclear nonproliferation. If we were now to condition certification on additional steps on chemical weapons and missiles, the Chinese would see this as moving the goalposts.

QUESTIONS FOR THE RECORD SUBMITTED TO ROBERT EINHORN
HOUSE INTERNATIONAL RELATIONS COMMITTEE
MARCH 4, 1998

General

Q.4. How credible is the Administration's assurance that nuclear cooperation with China would be suspended if there are future Chinese nuclear proliferation problems?

-- The Clinton Administration has argued that the Agreement would simply enable US firms to apply for export licenses and that US export control procedures would allow the United States to cut off nuclear sales in the event of future Chinese nuclear proliferation problems.

-- What credibility does the Administration have that it will cut off nuclear sales to China once the deals proceed and Export-Import Bank financing is committed, especially since the Administration did not sanction China in May 1996 after ring magnets were egregiously delivered to unsafeguarded Pakistani facilities?

A. In 1995 when we concluded that a Chinese entity had transferred a number of ring magnets to an unsafeguarded uranium enrichment facility in Pakistan, we moved promptly and aggressively to engage the Chinese on this matter. During the discussions, all ExIm Bank financing for China was suspended for a period of three months.

We have made clear to China that implementation of the US-China Nuclear Cooperation Agreement will depend on China's continued adherence to the May 1996 commitment not to provide assistance to unsafeguarded nuclear facilities and other assurances such as to engage in no new nuclear cooperation with Iran. We will continue to monitor China's behavior closely. The Chinese are aware that we can terminate nuclear trade with China if they do not abide by their commitments.

QUESTIONS FOR THE RECORD SUBMITTED TO ROBERT EINHORN
HOUSE INTERNATIONAL RELATIONS COMMITTEE
MARCH 4, 1998

China's Nuclear Program

Q.1. To what extent is China's nuclear power industry dependent upon outside suppliers?

-- Where does China currently obtain its non-indigenous nuclear-related equipment?

A. China has imported most of its civil nuclear reactor technology from other countries. The French firm, Framatome, has supplied two 984 Mwe power reactors at Daya Bay in Guandong. Framatome will also supply a replica of the Daya Bay reactors at Ling Ao. GE-Alsthrom will supply the turbines and other conventional equipment.

China has also concluded an agreement with Atomic Energy Company Limited (AECL) of Canada for a matched pair of 700 Mwe CANDU heavy water reactors to be built in Qinshan.

In addition, China has agreed to buy two Russian VVER-1000 reactors (the Russian version of the pressurized light water reactor) with a net output of about 950 Mwe each. Instrumentation and control are to be supplied by a yet-to-be-determined third party. China is also importing from Russia a centrifuge uranium enrichment facility.

The only indigenous reactor constructed thus far is the 280 MWE reactor, Qinshan 1, near Shanghai. However, much of the nuclear equipment used in its construction has been provided by foreign suppliers. The Japanese firm, Mitsubishi, supplied the pressure vessel and Siemens of Germany provided the primary coolant pumps. In addition, Framatome provided the reactor internals and instrumentation equipment.

QUESTIONS FOR THE RECORD SUBMITTED TO ROBERT EINHORN
HOUSE INTERNATIONAL RELATIONS COMMITTEE
MARCH 4, 1998

China's Nuclear Program

Q.2. What is the nature and extent of cooperation between China and other nuclear suppliers?

A. See the answer to question 1 immediately above.

QUESTIONS FOR THE RECORD SUBMITTED TO ROBERT EINHORN
HOUSE INTERNATIONAL RELATIONS COMMITTEE
MARCH 4, 1998

China's Nuclear Program

Q.3. How much cooperation do we receive from other nuclear suppliers in our efforts to moderate Chinese proliferation behavior?

A. We first approached the French, British and Germans in the early 1980s to urge them to refrain from entering nuclear cooperation with China until China ceased its support of the Pakistani nuclear weapons program. Since then, key members of the nonproliferation community, particularly European countries, have offered strong support to US positions within the context of nonproliferation regimes such as the Nuclear Suppliers Group (NSG), Missile Technology Control Regime (MTCR), Australia Group (AG) and Wassenaar Arrangement (WA).

These countries and other suppliers to China's civil nuclear program (Japan, Russia, and Canada) have urged the Chinese to adopt responsible nuclear export policies including adherence to the Guidelines of the Zangger Committee and the Nuclear Suppliers Group. The NSG's outreach activities have included many approaches to China which have encouraged adoption of the NSG guidelines. However, suppliers other than the US have not been willing to link their nuclear cooperation with China to improvements in Chinese export practices.

QUESTIONS FOR THE RECORD SUBMITTED TO ROBERT EINHORN
HOUSE INTERNATIONAL RELATIONS COMMITTEE
MARCH 4, 1998

China's Nuclear Program

Q.4. Is there a proliferation risk inherent in the technologies or resulting nuclear fuel provided by the US or other countries to China?

-- What are the risks of diversion internally to China's military nuclear infrastructure?

-- What about the risk of China diverting to other countries' nuclear programs?

A. For a number of reasons we believe that there is minimal risk of diversion to China's military program or to other countries' nuclear programs from the US-China Peaceful Nuclear Cooperation Agreement.

First, that Agreement does not permit cooperation under the Agreement in sensitive nuclear technology or restricted data. Special nuclear material transfers under the Agreement are restricted to low enriched uranium. (Plutonium and high enriched uranium may only be transferred in small quantities for use as samples, standards, detectors, etc.)

Second, China already has dedicated nuclear weapons facilities and has little incentive to divert the kinds of equipment, materials and technology that would be provided under this Agreement.

Third, the 1985 US-China Agreement contains a number of provisions that make diversion of US-supplied nuclear materials or equipment to China's nuclear weapons program highly unlikely. Paragraph 3 of Article 5 of the Agreement prohibits the use of any transferred material, facility or components for any nuclear explosive device, for research specifically on or development of any nuclear explosive device, or for any military purpose.

Paragraph 1 of Article 5 of the Agreement provides that retransfer of items subject to the Agreement may only take place with the prior consent of the United States.

Article 8 of the Agreement provides for the establishment of mutually acceptable arrangements for exchange of information and visits to material, facilities and components subject to the Agreement. We believe that the arrangements we have negotiated with the Chinese pursuant to Article 8 will provide the US with assurance that the items subject to the Agreement will be used only for their intended peaceful purposes.

China has also concluded agreements with other countries that contain similar peaceful use assurances and retransfer consent rights.

QUESTIONS FOR THE RECORD SUBMITTED TO ROBERT EINHORN
HOUSE INTERNATIONAL RELATIONS COMMITTEE
MARCH 4, 1998

China and the Multilateral Nonproliferation Regime

Q.1 As you well know, we did not succeed in requiring that China join the Nuclear Suppliers Group (NSG) as a condition for implementing the 1985 law.

-- Did the Administration formally ask China to join the NSG? Are there any reasons we would not want to have China as a member of the NSG?

A. The Administration has urged China to adhere to the NSG Guidelines and has discussed Chinese membership in NSG with Chinese officials. There are no reasons we would not want China to be a member of the NSG.

-- Would you agree that, along with the Nonproliferation Treaty (NPT) the NSG is one of the pillars on the international nonproliferation nuclear regime?

A. Yes.

-- Isn't it a central nonproliferation objective of this Administration to bring nuclear supplier nations, such as China, in the NSG?

A. We believe that the NSG would be most effective if it included in its membership every country that was capable of supplying nuclear trigger list or controlled dual-use items.

Over the years, the NSG has grown gradually from seven to 35 members, and the NSG is considering an additional two or three potential candidates for membership. China's admission to the Zangger Committee has shown its willingness to become a part of multilateral nonproliferation regimes. In the longer term, its admission to the NSG would be an additional indication of its support for such multilateral efforts.

> -- Don't you agree that China's unwillingness to join the NSG represents a glaring inconsistency between its nuclear nonproliferation commitment and prevailing international norms?

A. No. China's willingness to join the Zangger committee is an important step forward. It represents the first time China has participated in a multilateral nonproliferation export control regime. Committee membership will both enhance China's export control capabilities and strengthen its commitment to nonproliferation norms and practices. China was not willing to join the NSG at this time. We will continue to urge China to join the NSG. However, membership in the NSG is not required by the NPT and is not a requirement for nuclear certification.

> -- Once this Agreement is implemented what will be the leverage of the Administration to get China to join and adhere to the tenets of the NSG?

A. The implementation of the Agreement will give the Administration continuing opportunities to discuss nuclear nonproliferation issues with the Chinese. We plan to use these opportunities to discuss China's membership in the NSG. Other members can also be expected to urge China to join the NSG and to adhere to its tenets.

-- Please give examples of nuclear supplier countries with which we have implemented nuclear cooperation agreements that are not NSG members?

A. The United States presently has nuclear cooperation agreements in force with the following non-NSG countries: China, Colombia, Egypt, Indonesia, Morocco, Peru, the Philippines, and Thailand. The US has signed an agreement with one other non-NSG country - Kazakhstan. Of these countries, China and Kazakhstan would be considered supplier countries. Kazakhstan has expressed an interest in joining the NSG.

The United States has never made membership in the NSG a condition of nuclear cooperation.

-- Since China has not always played a constructive role in multilateral arms control fora in the past, how might China obstruct progress toward stricter nuclear export controls in the Zangger Committee? Is China likely to do so?

A. We do not expect that China would obstruct progress toward stricter nuclear export controls in the Zangger Committee. China's recent implementation of strict nuclear export controls and the positive bilateral dialogue we have had with China in this area are indicative of China's desire to work with the US and other countries to enhance the international nuclear nonproliferation regime.

QUESTIONS FOR THE RECORD SUBMITTED TO ROBERT EINHORN
HOUSE INTERNATIONAL RELATIONS COMMITTEE
MARCH 4, 1998

China and the Multilateral Nonproliferation Regime

Q. 2. I understand that China became a member of the Zangger Group in October 1997. Please explain to the Committee how Chinese membership in this group differs from the NSG.

-- Are you concerned that, given the fact the Zangger Group is committed to applying full-scope safeguards within three years, that Chinese membership in that group will derail this objective?

A. The NPT Exporters (Zangger) Committee was established to interpret Article III 2. of the NPT with respect to the requirement that nuclear transfers be subject to IAEA safeguards. The NSG, on the other hand, is not specifically linked to the NPT or any other treaty and therefore is much more flexible in its mandate. In this context, the NSG has established coordinated controls not only over nuclear items essentially parallel to those of the Zangger Committee, but also over nuclear-related dual-use exports and technology related to nuclear trigger list items. The NSG countries have also agreed to go beyond NPT requirements and require full-scope safeguards as a condition for nuclear supply.

There is no commitment on the part of the Zangger Committee to apply full-scope safeguards within any given deadline and a number of Zangger Committee members have taken the position that the NPT does not require a full-scope safeguards policy. The Zangger Committee is, however, discussing the question of adopting full-scope safeguards as a condition of supply as a matter of policy, and China is part of those discussions.

-- Does membership in the Zangger Group obligate China to do anything it is not already obligated to do?

A. No. The Guidelines and procedures of the Zangger Committee would not permit acceptance of a new member if that nation had not already met the requirements for membership, which are essentially that the nation be a party to the NPT, be a nuclear supplier, and have confirmed in writing that its export controls and policy are in conformity with the Zangger Committee Guidelines.

-- If not, is there any value to China's membership.

A. There is great value in China's membership in the Zangger Committee. The Zangger Committee is the first multilateral nonproliferation export control regime China has joined. This membership will enhance China's export control experience and strengthen its commitment to nonproliferation norms and practices. Upon joining, the Chinese representative issued a comprehensive statement regarding China's commitment to key nuclear export control principles, including no supply to unsafeguarded nuclear facilities or to any activity related to nuclear explosives and the requirement for Chinese consent for retransfer of supplied items to any third country.

QUESTIONS FOR THE RECORD SUBMITTED TO ROBERT EINHORN
HOUSE INTERNATIONAL RELATIONS COMMITTEE
MARCH 4, 1998

China and the Multilateral Nonproliferation Regime

Q.3. What would the probable Chinese reaction be if the Congress insisted that China join the NSG as a precondition for certification under the 1985 nuclear Agreement?

A. NSG membership includes a commitment by the parties to require full-scope safeguards in non-nuclear weapon states as a condition of significant nuclear supply. At this time, China is apparently unwilling to make that commitment, perhaps because of its nuclear cooperation with India and Pakistan. This cooperation is itself under safeguards, as the NPT and Zangger rules require, but India and Pakistan lack "full-scope" safeguards, i.e., safeguards on the entirety of their nuclear programs.

Full-scope safeguards as a condition of supply goes beyond the NPT, and was only adopted by the NSG in 1992. In our discussions with Chinese officials we have pressed them to adopt full-scope safeguards as a condition of supply, and we will continue to do so. But this is not a requirement for certification.

The United States has never required, either as a matter of law or policy, that its cooperating partners themselves require full-scope safeguards as a condition of supply. The NPT itself does not require it, nor did Congress make it a requirement for certification. We believe that the best way to encourage China to adopt a full-scope safeguards policy is through dialogue and cooperation, not by imposing new conditions on US nuclear exports to China.

QUESTIONS FOR THE RECORD SUBMITTED TO ROBERT EINHORN
HOUSE INTERNATIONAL RELATIONS COMMITTEE
MARCH 4, 1998

Chinese Export Controls

Q.1. The Administration notes that the Chinese State Council issued a "Circular" on nuclear export control policy in May 1997. The circular, or notice, was not promulgated as a set of regulations on dual-use nuclear trade.

--What is the legal authority of a circular and how is a circular different from regulations? Has China published the circular and the related list of dual-use nuclear items? Has the Administration seen the list?

A. On May 17, 1997 China's State Council issued a "Notice Regarding the Strict Implementation of China's Nuclear Export Control Policy". In the Chinese system, such a directive by the State Council has binding force. This Notice was supplemented in June by the issuance of a control list covering nuclear related dual-use items on the Nuclear Suppliers Group (NSG) dual-use list; the Chinese list is substantively identical to the NSG dual-use list.

The State Council directive states that nuclear exports will be controlled by the China National Nuclear Corporation, a governmental agency. No nuclear material, nuclear facility or technology, non-nuclear material used in a reactor, or nuclear-related dual-use equipment, material, and technology may be provided to or used in a nuclear facility that does not accept IAEA safeguards. In addition, the exchange of technical personnel or information is prohibited to facilities that do not accept safeguards.

A State Council decree is a common method by which Beijing informs government ministries, provincial governments, and government-owned and private industries of its policies. The Chinese have told us that they regard the May directive as providing binding, interim guidance pending promulgation of final, detailed regulations.

On September 10, the Ministry of Foreign Affairs announced the promulgation of China's nuclear export control regulations. These regulations were issued with a control list that is substantively identical to the Zangger Committee trigger list for nuclear items.

In the September announcement, Chinese officials also noted that they were working on nuclear-related dual-use regulations. They subsequently committed to promulgate these dual-use regulations in the first half of 1998, and in fact China announced the promulgation of those regulations on June 17, 1998.

The Administration has copies of both control lists in Chinese, and has translated them into English for comparison purposes. We have compared these lists to the NSG dual-use list and the Zangger Committee trigger list and have found them to be substantively identical.

QUESTIONS FOR THE RECORD SUBMITTED TO ROBERT EINHORN
HOUSE INTERNATIONAL RELATIONS COMMITTEE
MARCH 4, 1998

Chinese Export Controls

Q.2. China also issued export control regulations on nuclear trade--but not dual-use nuclear items--in September of 1997.

-- What are the short-comings of the Chinese nuclear export control system in general and the nuclear export control regulations in particular?

-- How concerned is the Administration that the Chinese Foreign Ministry, which represents China on nonproliferation matters, has no routine role in the review and approval process and does not have a right to suspend exports under the regulations?

-- How concerned is the Administration that China's Atomic Energy Authority (CAEA), one of the implementing agencies, is headed by the President of the China National Nuclear Corporation (CNNC), which has a conflicting interest in promoting nuclear exports?

A. Until 1997 China had not instituted comprehensive, nationwide regulations for the control of nuclear exports. Previously, some entities engaged in nuclear exports, generally nuclear-related dual-use exports, that were not subject to oversight by the Government of China.

China issued nuclear export control regulations in September 1997. In addition, on May 17, 1997 China issued a State Council "Notice Regarding the Strict Implementation of China's Nuclear Export Control Policy" which regulates nuclear-related, dual-use equipment and technology. This notice was supplemented in June, 1997 by the issuance of a control list covering nuclear dual-use items which is substantively identical to the Nuclear Suppliers Group (NSG) dual-use list. The Chinese told us that they regarded the May directive as providing binding, interim guidance pending promulgation of final, detailed regulations. Later in 1997 Chinese officials announced that they would issue formal nuclear-related dual-use regulations by mid-1998. China did in fact announce the promulgation of those regulations on June 17, 1998.

The Chinese Foreign Ministry has a role in the review process for nuclear exports. The nuclear export regulations issued in September specifically state that "In handling a nuclear export application that has important impact on national security, public interests, or diplomatic policy, the China Atomic Energy Authority, the State Commission of Science, Technology and Industry for National Defense as well as the Ministry of Foreign Trade and Economic Cooperation, should, during their reviews or reexaminations, consult with the Ministry of Foreign Affairs. If necessary, they should submit the case to the State Council for examination and approval."

In regard to suspending exports, the September regulations state that: "If the recipient or its government violates the guarantee made pursuant to the provisions of Article 5 of these regulations or if the danger of nuclear proliferation surfaces, the Ministry of Foreign Trade and Economic Cooperation, working jointly with the related departments of the State Council, will have the right to make the decision to discontinue export of related items or technologies." At the time these regulations were formulated, the Ministry of Foreign Affairs did not include the Arms Control Department. The Arms Control Department of MFA will be involved in nuclear export controls, especially in cases where proliferation is a risk.

The China Atomic Energy Authority and the China National Nuclear Corporation are currently headed by the same individual. We do not believe that this creates an obstacle to the implementation of nuclear export controls. The China Atomic Energy Authority reviews nuclear export applications and forwards a report to the State Commission of Science, Technology, and Industry for National Defense in the case of nuclear material or the Ministry of Foreign Trade and Economic Cooperation in the case of nuclear equipment or non-nuclear materials used for reactors and related technologies. These two authorities have the right to review the export. As previously explained, in certain cases, the Ministry of Foreign Affairs and the State Council can examine and approve or deny licenses.

QUESTIONS FOR THE RECORD SUBMITTED TO ROBERT EINHORN
HOUSE INTERNATIONAL RELATIONS COMMITTEE
MARCH 4, 1998

Chinese Export Controls

Q.3. Is there a track record of China's enforcement of its May 1997 circular and September 1997 regulations? Has the Chinese government stopped a pending sale because of concerns over nuclear proliferation since those were issued?

A. The May 1997 State Council directive highlighted China's policy of not assisting unsafeguarded nuclear facilities and included regulations over the export of nuclear-related dual-use items. In June, a control list substantively identical to the Nuclear Suppliers Group nuclear-related dual-use control list was issued.

The September 1997 State Council regulations on nuclear items included a nuclear control list substantively identical to the trigger list used by the Nuclear Suppliers Group.

The Administration understands the desire to see a track record; indeed, we have already acquired a substantial track record. We have been focusing very heavily on China's nuclear export activities in recent years, and since May 1996 have especially scrutinized its pledge not to assist unsafeguarded nuclear facilities. There is no basis to conclude that China has not abided by its commitments.

In recent months we encountered reports of a few potentially troubling contacts by Chinese entities or individuals with countries of concern. We raised these cases with the Chinese, pressed them to investigate, and urged that they prevent any transactions inconsistent with their assurances. In part, we believe, because of the incentives promised by implementation of the Agreement, the Chinese government conducted investigations and responded promptly to each of our inquiries. Our current information indicates that China is acting consistently with its stated policy of not assisting unsafeguarded nuclear facilities.

QUESTIONS FOR THE RECORD SUBMITTED TO ROBERT EINHORN
HOUSE INTERNATIONAL RELATIONS COMMITTEE
MARCH 4, 1998

Chinese Export Controls

Q.4. China had nuclear export control procedures in place in the past that were described, for example, in China's November 1995 white paper on arms control. How are the new export controls more effective than those in the past, which failed to control exports to unsafeguarded facilities?

A. China's November 1995 white paper on arms control states three principles governing China's nuclear exports: (1) such exports must be for peaceful use only; (2) IAEA safeguards must be applied to such exports; and (3) the items exported may not be retransferred to a third country without China's approval. However, the procedures to administer the policy, as described in the white paper, were much more rudimentary than those that China has recently adopted in the context of the US-China discussions leading toward implementation of the US-China Agreement for Peaceful Nuclear Cooperation. In fact, in terms of internal Chinese government procedures, the white paper merely notes that only specialized government-designated companies can handle nuclear exports, and that in each instance they must apply for approval from relevant government departments.

By contrast, and at least in part as a result of our intensive dialogue with China on effective export control procedures in the context of meeting conditions for implementation of the US-China Agreement for Cooperation, China is now putting in place for the first time a comprehensive, nationwide system of nuclear and nuclear-related dual-use export controls. This system is much more concrete and detailed than the one referred to in the white paper, both as regards the items subject to control, the process for approval of exports, and the consequences for failure to implement the controls in a proper manner. The new system includes such features as:

-- Placing all nuclear exports under the control of the State Atomic Energy Agency, whose responsibility it is to examine all nuclear export applications and refer them to other government agencies as necessary.

-- Control lists for nuclear and nuclear-related dual-use commodities that are substantively identical with the Nuclear Suppliers Group lists.

-- Coverage of technology in all forms, including exchanges of personnel and information.

-- A requirement that exporters of nuclear-related dual-use items to non-NPT countries seek prior confirmation from

China's Atomic Energy Authority of the IAEA safeguards status of nuclear facilities in the recipient country, and end-user certificates from the importing government along with assurances against diversion to unsafeguarded facilities.

-- A "case-by-case" authority similar to "catch-all" whereby exports that pose a proliferation risk, whether or not they are on a control list, will be denied export licenses.

-- Authority for taking criminal, civil or administrative actions against violators of the regulations.

QUESTIONS FOR THE RECORD SUBMITTED TO ROBERT EINHORN
HOUSE INTERNATIONAL RELATIONS COMMITTEE
MARCH 4, 1998

Chinese Export Controls

Q.5. China has increasingly argued--and the Clinton Administration has concurred--that the Chinese government is not responsible for and cannot control all sensitive exports (e.g., the ring magnets to unsafeguarded Pakistani facilities, exports to Iranian chemical weapon program).

-- How much control does the Chinese government have over its defense-related state-owned-enterprises, such as the China National Nuclear Corporation (CNNC)? If the Chinese government does lack effective control over its state-owned conglomerates, how meaningful are any new export control regulations?

A. The Chinese government currently has control over the defense-related state-owned enterprises, including CNNC. This control may weaken as the Chinese government continues to restructure the bureaucracy and the economy. We have urged the government to take steps to maintain effective controls as restructuring progresses.

As discussed elsewhere, China issued an Interim Directive on nuclear export controls in May 1997, and a nuclear export control regulation in September 1997. The US government consulted with the Chinese on the new regulations, providing assistance as requested. On June 17, 1998, China announced the promulgation of the nuclear-related dual-use regulations.

While the new export control regulations give the central Beijing government control over exports, it is possible that increasing economic pressure on deregulated enterprises could lead individuals to be in contact with foreign colleagues with whom they have had long established relationships in programs of concern and attempt to circumvent the regulations. We have urged the Chinese government to monitor closely any attempts to circumvent the regulations. We have no basis to conclude that China has not kept its international nuclear commitments, including its commitment not to assist unsafeguarded facilities.

Question for the Record submitted to Robert Einhorn
House International Relations Committee
March 4, 1998

Chinese Export Controls

7. Is China currently abiding by the provisions of the Australia Group?

Answer:

China is not a member of the Australia Group and has made no commitments to observe the specific provisions of the Australia Group.

QUESTIONS FOR THE RECORD SUBMITTED TO ROBERT EINHORN
HOUSE INTERNATIONAL RELATIONS COMMITTEE
MARCH 4, 1998

Chinese Export Controls

Q.9. Will China apply in practice the broad definition of "assistance" to include personnel exchanges and technology sharing arrangements in its nuclear export controls?

-- Has China specifically prohibited assistance to nuclear explosive programs in its May 1996 statement and in its September 1997 regulations?

-- Shouldn't the US insist at a minimum that China issue a comprehensive export control law that includes regulation on nuclear trade and dual-use nuclear items before we provide a wide range of nuclear export licenses to China? As presently drafted, the regulations do not cover dual-use nuclear exports and China has said that it will not even issue regulations for these items until the middle of this year.

A. China already has in effect controls for the export of nuclear technology and nuclear-related dual-use items. These controls are binding on all entities in China. Moreover, on June 17, 1998, China announced the promulgation of dual-use controls. A copy of these regulations is attached.

China began its adoption of dual-use controls in a May 17, 1997 State Council "Notice Regarding the Strict Implementation of China's Nuclear Export Control Policy". In the Chinese system, such a directive by the State Council has binding force.

This Notice was supplemented in June, 1997 by the issuance of a list of controlled nuclear dual-use items; this list is substantively identical to the Nuclear Suppliers Group (NSG) dual-use list. The September nuclear regulations were supplemented by a control list that is substantively identical to the Zangger Committee trigger list.

The State Council directive states that nuclear exports will be controlled by the China National Nuclear Corporation, a government agency. No nuclear material, nuclear facility or technology, non-nuclear material used in a reactor, or nuclear related dual-use equipment, material, and technology may be provided to a recipient for use in a nuclear facility that does not accept IAEA safeguards. In addition, the exchange of technical personnel or information is prohibited to facilities that do not accept safeguards. China has made clear that these regulations apply not only to unsafeguarded nuclear facilities but to all activities related to nuclear explosives.

A State Council decree is a common method by which Beijing informs government ministries, provincial governments, and government-owned and private industries of its policies. The Chinese have told us that they regard the May directive as providing binding, interim guidance pending promulgation of final, detailed regulations.

On September 10,1997, the Ministry of Foreign Affairs announced the promulgation of China's nuclear control regulations. In this announcement, they also noted that they were working on nuclear-related dual-use regulations. A copy of these regulations is attached. They subsequently committed to promulgate these dual-use regulations in the first half of 1998. As noted above, on June 17, 1998, China announced the adoption of nuclear-related dual-use controls.

SUBJ: Take 1 of 2 -- Nuclear Product Export Controls Issued

SOURCE: Beijing Xinhua Domestic Service in Chinese 0301 GMT 17 Jun 98

TEXT:

[PRC Regulations for Controlling the Export of Dual-Purpose Nuclear Goods and Relevant Technologies]

[FBIS Translated Text] Beijing, 17 Jun (Xinhua) -- PRC Regulations for Controlling the Export of Dual-Purpose Nuclear Goods and Relevant Technologies

Article 1. These regulations are drawn up for the purpose of tightening control over the export of dual-purpose nuclear goods and correlated technologies [he liang yong pin ji xiang guan ji shu 2702 0357 3938 0756 0644 4161 7070 2111 2611], preventing the proliferation of nuclear weapons, promoting international cooperation on the peaceful use of nuclear energy, and safeguarding national security and public interests.

Article 2. The phrase -- export of dual-purpose nuclear goods and correlated technologies -- used in these regulations refers to the commercial export of equipment, materials, and correlated technologies, which are listed in the annex of these regulations -- the "Export Control Inventory of Dual-Purpose Nuclear Goods and Correlated Technologies" (referred to as "Control Inventory" below); as well as the acts of giving them to foreign countries as gifts, exhibiting them, and using them for scientific-technological cooperation and assistance programs.

Article 3. The state exercises strict control over the export of dual-purpose nuclear goods and correlated technologies, and strictly abides by the international obligations it undertakes of not proliferating nuclear weapons.

Article 4. The export of dual-purpose nuclear goods and correlated technologies shall abide by the relevant state laws and administrative regulations as well as the rules of these regulations; and it shall not jeopardize national security and public interests.

Article 5. The state implements the system of licensing the export of dual-purpose nuclear goods and correlated technologies.

Article 6. The licensing of the export of dual-purpose nuclear goods and correlated technologies shall abide by the following guidelines:

(1) The recipient side guarantees not to use the dual-purpose nuclear goods and correlated technologies from China for conducting nuclear explosions;

(2) The recipient side guarantees not to use the dual-purpose nuclear goods and correlated technologies from China on nuclear facilities not safeguarded and supervised by the International Nuclear Energy Agency; and

(3) The recipient side guarantees not to transfer to a third party the dual purpose nuclear goods and correlated technologies from China.

Article 7. Operators engaged in exporting dual-purpose nuclear goods and correlated technologies shall register at the Ministry of Foreign Trade and Economic Cooperation [MOFTEC]. No unregistered unit or individual may export dual-purpose nuclear goods and correlated technologies. MOFTEC shall draw up specific registration procedures.

Article 8. To export dual-purpose nuclear goods and correlated technologies listed in the "Control Inventory," an application shall be submitted to the MOFTEC. In addition to filling in the Dual-Purpose Nuclear Goods and Correlated Technologies Export Form (referred to as Export Application Form below), the following documents shall also be submitted:

(1) Papers certifying the identities of the applicant's legal representative and principal operator, as well as the person who handles the application;

(2) A copy of contract or agreement;

(3) The manual that explains the dual-purpose nuclear goods and correlated technologies;

(4) Certificate of the terminal purchaser;

(5) Vouchers prescribed in Article 6; and

(6) Other documents MOFTEC requires.

Article 9. If the dual-purpose nuclear goods and correlated technologies to be exported are goods and technologies for exhibition overseas, or for China's own use overseas and will be shipped back to China within a prescribed period, the documents prescribed in Article 8 may be exempted with MOFTEC concurrence.

Article 10. The applicant shall fill in the Export Application Form factually. MOFTEC prints the Export Application Form uniformly.

Article 11. MOFTEC, beginning from the day it receives the Export Application Form and documents prescribed in Article 8, shall work with the National Nuclear Energy Agency, or with the agency and relevant State Council departments -- and also with the Ministry of Foreign Affairs if foreign policy is involved -- to review the application and make a decision of approving or disapproving the application within 45 working days.

(more) 170301 cc/djuric

ST
13989
NNNN

SUBJ: Take 2 of 2 -- Nuclear Product Export Controls Issued

REF: OW1906115998 Beijing Xinhua Domestic Service in Chinese 0301 GMT 17 ///45 working days.

TEXT:

[FBIS Translated Text] Article 12. For the export of dual-purpose nuclear goods and correlated technologies that have a major impact on national security, public interests, and foreign policy, MOFTEC shall refer the application to the State Council for approval. Cases referred to the State Council for approval are not subjected to the time limit restraint prescribed in Article 11 of these regulations.

Article 13. For the application for exporting dual-purpose nuclear goods and correlated technologies that has been reviewed and approved, MOFTEC shall issue it a License for the Export of Dual-Purpose Nuclear Goods and Correlated Technologies (to be called license below), and notify the customs administration in writing.

Article 14. In case the license sponsor has to change the dual-purpose nuclear goods and correlated technologies he had applied for export, he shall return the license that has been issued, and apply a new license according to the rules in these regulations.

Article 15. While exporting dual-purpose nuclear goods and correlated technologies, the exporter shall show the license to the customs office, process the necessary formalities according to the Customs Law, and accept the customs office's supervision.

Article 16. If the recipient side violates the guarantees it has made according to Article 6 of these regulations, or should nuclear proliferation risks appear, MOFTEC, after consulting with the Ministry of Foreign Affairs and the National Nuclear Energy Agency, shall terminate or revoke the license that has been issued, and notify the customs office in writing for action.

Article 17. With the State Council's approval, MOFTEC, working with relevant State Council departments, may make an ad hoc decision of exercising control over the export of specific dual-purpose nuclear goods and correlated technologies not listed in the Control Inventory.

The export of specific dual-purpose nuclear goods and correlated technologies prescribed in the clause above shall be licensed according to rules of these regulations.

Article 18. Anyone who exports dual-purpose nuclear goods and correlated technologies in violation of these regulations, and whose conduct constitutes a crime, shall have his criminal responsibilities investigated according to the law; or punished according to the regulations of the Foreign Trade Law and Customs Law if the conduct does not constitute a crime.

Article 19. Anyone who counterfeits, alters, buys, or sells an export license shall have his legal liabilities investigated according to the law.

Article 20. State functionaries in charge of control over the export of dual-purpose nuclear goods and correlated technologies shall have their criminal responsibilities investigated according to the law if their conduct of neglecting their duties, playing favoritism, committing irregularities, or abusing their authority constitutes a crime; and if their conduct does not constitute a crime, they shall be disciplined according to the law.

Article 21. MOFTEC may work with the National Nuclear Energy Agency and relevant State Council departments to adjust the Control Inventory according to actual circumstances and report the adjustments to the State Council for approval.

Article 22. If international treaties which the PRC has signed, or has acceded to, have different provisions that differ from these regulations, the provisions in the international treaties shall apply, except for those provisions for which the PRC had stated reservation.

Article 23. These regulations become effective upon promulgation.

(Export Control Inventory of Dual-Purpose Nuclear Goods and Correlated Technologies omitted)

[Description of source: Beijing Xinhua Domestic Service in Chinese -- China's official news service (New China News Agency)]

(endall) 170301 cc/djuric
BT
#3950
NNNN

460

RUEKJCS/SECDEF WASHINGTON DC
RUERPMB/CDRJOTC T SHERMAN PM//SOJT-SB/S-2//
RUESDG/PTS HONG KONG
RUESDP/FBIS SEOUL KOR
RUETIAV/MPC FT GEO G MEAE MD
RUFQBBA/SURVEY DIV SHAPE BE
RUHDDMM/6924EG KUNIA HI//DOM//
RUHDFTB/CDRUSAFLDSTA OPS KUNIA I
RUHDKAN/NAVSECGRUACT KUNIA HI
RUHDTSN/THEATE SUPPORT NODE PACIFIC HI
RUKWKAD/82RS OKINAWA JA/DOI//
RUWTAEA/NAIC WRIGHT PATTERSN AFB OH
RUYLBAH/DODSPECREP OKINAWA JA
ACCT FBOW-EDWK
BT
UNCLAS 1K

AC

WARNING: USVIENNA: IAEA

WARNING: USVIENNA: ASG

WARNING: GENEVA: ARMS CONTROL

WARNING: TOPIC: ENERGY, INTERNATIONAL, POLITICAL, TECHNOLOGY

SERIAL: OW1309060397
PASS: COPY TO GSG/TAC

COUNTRY: CHINA
SUBJ: Take 1 of 2 -- PRC Regulations on Nuclear Exports

REF: 1. ow1209004897 service -- prc regulations on nuclear exports
2. wa1109235697 service -- further interest in decree on nuclear exports
3. ow1109232297 beijing xinhua english 111753 -- li peng signs decree regulating nuclear exports

SOURCE: Beijing Xinhua Domestic Service in Chinese 0917 GMT 11 Sep 97

TEXT:

[FBIS Translated Text] Beijing, 11 Sep (Xinhua) -- The Regulations of the People's Republic of China on Control of Nuclear Exports.

Article 1. These regulations are formulated for the purpose of tightening control over nuclear exports, safeguarding national security and public interests, and promoting international cooperation in peaceful utilization of nuclear energy.

Article 2. The term nuclear exports used hereinafter refers to trading-related exports, gifts to and exhibitions in foreign countries, as well as scientific and technological cooperation with and assistance to foreign countries that involve nuclear materials, nuclear equipment, non-nuclear materials used for reactors, and other items as well as their related technologies, as listed in the attachment, entitled "Nuclear Exports Control List" (hereinafter referred to as "Control List"), to these regulations.

Article 3. The state tightly controls nuclear exports and strictly performs the international obligation on non-proliferation of nuclear weapons it has undertaken.

The state does not advocate, encourage and engage in proliferation of nuclear weapons, and does not help other countries develop nuclear weapons. Nuclear exports are used only for peaceful purposes and are subjected to International Atomic Energy Agency's guarantee and supervision. Without the Chinese Government's approval, the recipient is not allowed to make transfer to a third country. The state prohibits assistance to nuclear facilities not subject to International Atomic Energy Agency's guarantee and supervision, and does not engage in nuclear exports or personnel and technological exchanges and cooperation with them.

Article 4. Nuclear exports should follow the provisions of the state's relevant laws and administrative decrees without jeopardizing national security or public interests.

Article 5. The following principles should be observed in examining and approving nuclear exports:

1. The recipient government guarantees not to use for nuclear explosion purposes China-supplied nuclear materials, nuclear equipment, or non-nuclear materials used for reactors as well as special kind of fissile materials produced through the use of the said materials and equipment;

2. The recipient government guarantees to take appropriate measures to physically protect China-supplied nuclear materials as well as the special kind of fissile materials produced through the use of the nuclear materials;

3. The recipient government has concluded a valid guarantee and supervision agreement with IAEA, promises to include in that agreement China-supplied nuclear materials, nuclear equipment, or non-nuclear materials used for reactors as well as special kind of fissile materials produced through the use of the said nuclear materials and equipment, and accepts IAEA's guarantee and supervision;

4. The recipient guarantees that, without prior written approval by China Atomic Energy Authority, it will not transfer to a third party China-supplied nuclear materials, nuclear equipment or non-nuclear materials used for reactors as well as their related technologies. If prior approval is given to the transfer, the third party that accepts the transfer should undertake commitments corresponding to those of the recipient directly supplied by China.

Article 6. Nuclear exports shall be monopolized by units designated by the State Council. Other units or individuals are not allowed to handle nuclear exports.

Article 7. To export items listed on the "Control List" and their related technologies, it is necessary to apply to China Atomic Energy Authority, fill in the Nuclear Export Application form, and submit the following documents:

1. The applicant's certificate of monopoly in nuclear exports;
2. The identification of the applicant's legal representative, the primary executives and the administrators;
3. Duplicate copy of the contract or agreement;
4. Analysis report on nuclear materials or non-nuclear materials used for reactors;
5. Certificate of the final end-user;
6. Certificate of guarantee by the recipient as required by Article 5 of these regulations;
7. Other documents required by the examining agency.

Article 8. Applicant should truthfully fill out the Nuclear Export Application form. The Nuclear Export Application form will be centrally printed by China Atomic Energy Authority.

Article 9. If changes are to be made to the items entered in the Nuclear Export Application form, the applicant should promptly submit revisions, or resubmit the export application.

(more) 110917 fs/morriss
BT
#7678
NNNN

COUNTRY: CHINA
SUBJ: Take 2 of 2 -- PRC Regulations on Nuclear Exports

REF: OW1309060397 Beijing Xinhua Domestic Service in Chinese 0917 GMT 11 ///the export application.

TEXT:

[FBIS Translated Text] Applicants who discontinue nuclear exports should promptly withdraw their export applications.

Article 10. Within 15 working days after receiving the Nuclear Export Application form and the documents required by Article 7 of these regulations, the China Atomic Energy Authority shall submit a review report and notify the applicant. If approval is given after the review, the following procedures should be followed, according to different circumstances:

1. Export of nuclear materials shall be forwarded to the State Commission of Science, Technology, and Industry for National Defense for reexamination;

2. Export nuclear equipment or non-nuclear materials used for reactors as well as their related technologies shall be forwarded to the Ministry of Foreign Trade and Economic Cooperation for reexamination or the ministry will jointly reexamine the case with the State Commission of Science, Technology and Industry for National Defense.

Within 15 working days after receiving the nuclear exports

application form, the documents required by Article 7 of these regulations, and the review report forwarded by China Atomic Energy Authority, the State Commission of Science, Technology and Industry for National Defense, and the Ministry of Foreign Trade and Economic Cooperation shall submit a reexamination report and notify the applicant.

Under special circumstances, if the China Atomic Energy Authority, the State Commission of Science, Technology and Industry for National Defense, as well as the Ministry of Foreign Trade and Economic Cooperation need to extend the review or reexamination period, they can extend it for another 15 working days. But they should notify the applicant.

Article 11. In handling a nuclear export application that has important impact on national security, public interests, or diplomatic policy, the China Atomic Energy Authority, the State Commission of Science, Technology and Industry for National Defense as well as the Ministry of Foreign Trade and Economic Cooperation should, during their reviews or reexaminations, consult with the Ministry of Foreign Affairs. If necessary, they should submit the case to the State Council for examination and approval.

Cases submitted to the State Council for examination and approval shall not be restricted by the time limit stipulated in Article 10 of these regulations.

Article 12. For Nuclear Export Applications that have been approved after examination and reexamination as stipulated by these regulations, the Ministry of Foreign Trade and Economic Cooperation shall issue a Nuclear Export Permit.

Article 13. Bearers of a Nuclear Export Permit who change the items and related technologies on the original export applications should turn in their original permits, and follow the provisions of these regulations to file a new application and obtain Nuclear Export Permit.

Article 14. After issuing the Nuclear Export Permit, the Ministry of Foreign Trade and Economic Cooperation shall notify China Atomic Energy Authority in writing.

Article 15. Before a monopoly nuclear exporter carries out nuclear export, it should submit the Nuclear Export Permit to the Customs, follow the customs formalities stipulated in the Customs Law, and be subjected to the Customs' supervision and control.

Article 16. If the recipient or its government violates the guarantee made pursuant to the provisions of Article 5 of these regulations or if the danger of nuclear proliferation surfaces, the Ministry of Foreign Trade and Economic Cooperation, working jointly with the related departments of the State Council, will have the right to make the decision to discontinue export of related items or technologies. Yhe Ministry of Foreign Trade and Economic Cooperation shall notify the Customs in writing to enforce that decision.

Article 17. Those who violate the provisions of these regulations in exporting nuclear materials, nuclear equipment, non-nuclear materials used for reactors and their related technologies, thereby constituting a crime, shall be held accountable for their criminal responsibilities according to the law; those that do not constitute a crime shall be penalized according to the provisions of the Customs Law and the Law on Foreign Trade.

Article 18. Those who forge, alter, buy and sell Nuclear Export Permits shall be held accountable for their criminal responsibilities.

Article 19. Working personnel of the state's export control agencies who neglect their duties, commit fraud to seek private gains, or abuse their power, thereby constituting a crime, shall be held accountable for their criminal responsibilities; administrative disciplinary actions shall be taken against those whose actions do not constitute a crime.

Article 20. In light of the practical situation, China Atomic Energy Authority, together with the State Commission of Science, Technology and Industry for National Defense, the Ministry of Foreign Trade and Economic Cooperation, the Ministry of Foreign Affairs, the General Administration of Customs, and other departments, may readjust the "Control List" and submit it to the State Council for approval before implementation.

Article 21. If an international treaty that the People's Republic of China concluded or participated in contains provisions different than those of these regulations, the provisions of the international treaty shall apply; however, this does not apply to articles for which the People's Republic of China has declared its reservations.

Article 22. These regulations shall go into effect on the day of issue. (The "Nuclear Export Control List" omitted)

(endall) 110917 fs/morriss
BT
#7679
NNNN

QUESTIONS FOR THE RECORD SUBMITTED TO ROBERT EINHORN
HOUSE INTERNATIONAL RELATIONS COMMITTEE
MARCH 4, 1998

Chinese Export Controls

Q.11. Maintaining a tight system of export controls requires three things: good laws, an effective regulatory mechanism to enforce the laws, and political will. Please comment on each of these three things with respect to China's nuclear, missile, and chemical weapons exports? How plausible is it that senior Chinese leaders would not be informed of potentially controversial Chinese nuclear, missile, or chemical weapons exports prior to the export occurring?

A. The Chinese have told us that they have been working on the export control regulations for a number of years. They appear to be taking the matter seriously. The nuclear export control regulations were implemented effective September 10, 1997.

The new nuclear export control regulations control essentially the same items controlled by other nuclear suppliers using the internationally recognized Zangger Committee "trigger list".

The regulations contain key features essential to an effective export control system, including criminal and administrative penalties for violations, and a provision for cut-off of any end-user or government that contravenes any guarantee that it makes to China in order to obtain a nuclear export permit.

Although the detailed nuclear regulations took formal effect only on September 10, 1997, the interim directive on nuclear-related dual-use items took effect on May 17, 1997. On June 17, 1998, China announced the promulgation of nuclear-related dual-use regulations. Moreover, we have seen determined Chinese efforts to tighten their export control procedures since May 1996 when they committed not to assist unsafeguarded nuclear facilities.

We have followed these efforts closely and have no basis to conclude that the Chinese have acted inconsistently with their commitments.

Thus we now have a period of nearly two years in which we have evaluated Chinese nuclear export control behavior against very high standards.

It is unlikely that senior Chinese officials would not be informed of a potentially controversial export closely related to nuclear weapons prior to the export occurring. However, given the size of the country, the rapidly changing economic climate, and the economic restructuring taking place, it is possible that senior officials would not be aware of all nuclear exports, especially in the nuclear-related dual-use area. Our recent experience indicates that once a potentially questionable export has been identified to the Chinese authorities, they have investigated the report rapidly and shared their conclusions with us.

QUESTIONS FOR THE RECORD SUBMITTED TO ROBERT EINHORN
HOUSE INTERNATIONAL RELATIONS COMMITTEE
MARCH 4, 1998

China's Nuclear Assistance to Iran

Q.2. According to press reports that are confirmed by Administration officials, on the eve of the summit in October, 1997, Chinese Foreign Minister Qian Qichen provided a secret letter to Secretary of State Madeleine Albright promising not to begin new nuclear cooperation explicitly with Iran. Officials say that the letter may be shown to Members of Congress.

-- Do the refusals of China's President and Foreign Minister while in Washington to disavow nuclear assistance to Iran publicly reflect yet another example in a long record of weak assurances on nonproliferation? Why cannot the Chinese promise be made public? Is there concern that China will renege on this assurance as it has reneged on assurances in the past, such as those on missile proliferation?

A. We have received an assurance from China that it will not engage in new nuclear cooperation with Iran and will complete existing projects (which are not of proliferation concern) in a relatively short period of time. We regard this assurance as firm and believe that the Chinese reluctance to make it publicly relates more to their relationship with Iran than to the commitment they have made to us. We fully expect the Chinese to abide by their assurance to refrain from new nuclear cooperation with Iran. That said, we will closely monitor China's contacts with Iran.

QUESTIONS FOR THE RECORD SUBMITTED TO ROBERT EINHORN
HOUSE INTERNATIONAL RELATIONS COMMITTEE
MARCH 4, 1998

Chinese Nuclear Assistance to Iran

Q.3. What explains China's apparent retreat since 1995 in nuclear cooperation with Iran? Is China's curtailment of nuclear cooperation with Iran tied to US implementation of the Nuclear Cooperation Agreement?

-- Is the curtailment the result of various factors, including competition from Russia's sale of reactors, concerns of Israel (a key supplier to China's military), a desire to improve US-China relations, Iran's financial problems, and increasing recognition by Beijing that stability in the Middle East and in oil prices helps China's economy?

-- Is China's curtailment a meaningful change of policy to stop its activities which lead to nuclear proliferation?

A. We believe that the Chinese government weighed many factors in assessing the benefits of their safeguarded nuclear cooperation with Iran against the benefits of peaceful nuclear cooperation with the US and decided that it was in their best interest to forego cooperation with Iran. It is not possible to explain exactly which factors led the Chinese to make the decision, but it is apparent that one factor was China's desire to improve the US-China relationship.

China's curtailment of nuclear cooperation with Iran is definitely tied to US implementation of the 1985 Agreement. During discussions on implementation of the Agreement, the

US urged China (as we have urged all other nuclear suppliers) to refrain from any such cooperation because of our concerns that Iran is seeking nuclear weapons and our belief that even safeguarded cooperation could contribute to that effort.

A number of decisions taken by China over the last few years point to a meaningful change in China's nonproliferation policy. China adhered to the NPT in 1992 and in 1995 supported its indefinite and unconditional extension. China terminated nuclear testing and signed the Comprehensive Test Ban Treaty, supported the Fissile Material Cutoff Treaty, and supported the strengthened safeguards system of the IAEA. China has played a helpful role in achieving the Agreed Framework with North Korea.

QUESTIONS FOR THE RECORD SUBMITTED TO ROBERT EINHORN
HOUSE INTERNATIONAL RELATIONS COMMITTEE
MARCH 4, 1998

Chinese Nuclear Assistance to Pakistan

Q.3. Is China enforcing its nuclear export controls to include all types of "assistance," including technological, scientific, and personnel exchanges?

A. Yes, the State Council Directive issued in May, 1997 states that nuclear exports will be controlled by the China National Nuclear Corporation, a governmental agency. No nuclear material, nuclear facility or technology, non-nuclear material used in a reactor, or nuclear-related dual-use equipment, material, and technology may be provided to or used in a nuclear facility that does not accept IAEA safeguards. In addition, the exchange of technical personnel or information is prohibited to facilities that do not accept safeguards.

50-151 98 - 7

QUESTIONS FOR THE RECORD SUBMITTED TO ROBERT EINHORN
HOUSE INTERNATIONAL RELATIONS COMMITTEE
MARCH 4, 1998

Chinese Nuclear Assistance to Pakistan

Q.4. What are the details of reported concerns of US intelligence regarding China's assistance to Pakistan's nuclear weapon program?

-- Does the Administration consider Chinese weapon-related assistance to Pakistan to be less dangerous than China's assistance to Iran?

A. The United States is strongly opposed to any assistance that could contribute to any non-nuclear weapon state's efforts to acquire a nuclear weapons capability. Pakistan and Iran are in different stages of their nuclear weapons program. Pakistan has already detonated a number of nuclear devices. Any Chinese assistance to Pakistan's nuclear weapons program at this point would raise grave concerns, would constitute a violation of the Treaty on Nonproliferation of Nuclear Weapons (NPT), would directly contravene Chinese assurances to the US regarding China's nuclear policy, and would seriously undermine the international nonproliferation regime.

Iran is still in the early stages of its nuclear weapons program. Our concern was that Chinese assistance to Iran's nuclear program--even under safeguards--could over time contribute to Iran's nuclear weapons ambitions by providing Iran a more robust nuclear infrastructure.

QUESTIONS FOR THE RECORD SUBMITTED TO ROBERT EINHORN
HOUSE INTERNATIONAL RELATIONS COMMITTEE
MARCH 4, 1998

Chinese Nuclear Assistance to Pakistan

Q.6. What sort of assistance does China provide Pakistan's safeguarded facilities?

-- Is all this assistance compliant with China's NPT obligations?

-- What steps has China taken to prevent unauthorized or illegal disclosures in interactions with Pakistani technicians ostensibly affiliated with safeguarded Pakistani facilities?

-- Do we think these steps are adequate?

A. Current safeguarded assistance to Pakistan includes the construction of the 300 MW Chasma power reactor and related assistance, and the supply of heavy water for the safeguarded Kanupp power reactor. This assistance is in keeping with China's NPT obligations.

This question has been answered in further detail in the classified responses.

QUESTIONS FOR THE RECORD SUBMITTED TO ROBERT EINHORN
HOUSE INTERNATIONAL RELATIONS COMMITTEE
MARCH 4, 1998

Additional Questions from Representative Gilman

1. Has China committed to putting "catch-all" export controls in place similar to the Enhanced Proliferation Control Initiative (EPCI) regulation that the US and many other MTCR and NSG members have adopted?

A. China has stated that it is pursuing catch-all controls over nuclear-related dual-use exports. However, we do not have details regarding these controls and expect that they may be quite different from US EPCI controls. There is no international standard for catch-all controls nor are catch-all controls a requirement for any multilateral nonproliferation regime. Not all NSG members have catch-all controls and we know that EU member catch-all controls have significant differences from ours.

Now that China has announced the promulgation of its new dual-use controls, we will be examining them closely, particularly with regard to catch-all controls.

QUESTIONS FOR THE RECORD SUBMITTED TO ROBERT EINHORN
HOUSE INTERNATIONAL RELATIONS COMMITTEE
MARCH 4, 1998

Additional Questions from Representative Gilman

2. Is China likely to adopt EPCI-like regulations before or after it adopts dual-use nuclear regulations in the middle of this year?

A. We will be examining China's new dual-use controls to ascertain if they contain a form of EPCI-type controls. As stated in the response to the previous question, many countries now have catch-all controls and China has committed to adopt such controls, but there is no multilateral obligation to adopt EPCI-type catch-all controls.

QUESTIONS FOR THE RECORD SUBMITTED TO ROBERT EINHORN
HOUSE INTERNATIONAL RELATIONS COMMITTEE
MARCH 4, 1998

Additional Questions from Representative Gilman

3. When would the EPCI controls be legally binding on Chinese entities? Could China effectively enforce and fully implement all of the export control commitments it has made to the US with an EPCI-like regime in place?

A. China has committed to adopt catch-all controls over its dual-use exports but there is no international or multilateral obligation for China to adopt US EPCI-type controls. Although China's export control system is relatively new, China has already demonstrated a commitment to make it work effectively. We believe that Chinese export controls can be effective without necessarily adopting measures identical to EPCI.

QUESTIONS FOR THE RECORD SUBMITTED TO ROBERT EINHORN
HOUSE INTERNATIONAL RELATIONS COMMITTEE
MARCH 4, 1998

Questions from Representative Berman

Q.1. Has China ever provided the US with assurances that it would not cooperate with other countries in safeguarded uranium enrichment or nuclear reprocessing activities?

A. No, and we have not sought such assurances from China, recognizing that not all nuclear suppliers have a policy of refraining from cooperation in uranium enrichment or nuclear reprocessing activities. Members of the Nuclear Suppliers Group, however, have agreed on the Nuclear Suppliers Guidelines to exercise "restraint" with respect to the transfer of such technology.

QUESTIONS FOR THE RECORD SUBMITTED TO ROBERT EINHORN
HOUSE INTERNATIONAL RELATIONS COMMITTEE
MARCH 4, 1998

Questions from Representative Berman

Q2. How will China's joining the Zangger Group likely affect the ability of that group to reach consensus on the need for group members to require full-scope safeguards as a nuclear supply policy?

A. The Zangger Committee has frequently discussed the question of adoption of a full-scope safeguards policy, and in October 1997 convened an open-ended group to continue exploring the issue. There is no requirement for the Committee to adopt such a policy since the NPT does not require full-scope safeguards as a condition of nuclear supply. It would be premature to speculate on what position China will ultimately adopt within the Zangger Group.

QUESTIONS FOR THE RECORD SUBMITTED TO ROBERT EINHORN
HOUSE INTERNATIONAL RELATIONS COMMITTEE
MARCH 4, 1998

Questions from Representative Berman

Q.3. Does China have any nuclear nonproliferation laws that require the imposition of a sanction against another country or foreign person that engages in any illicit nuclear weapons-related activity? Does China, for example, have any laws requiring sanctions against any non-nuclear-weapon state that detonates a nuclear device, imports or exports such a device or design information or components thereof, traffics in sensitive fuel cycle technology, or assists a terrorist group to acquire a nuclear device?

A. We are not aware that China has any laws that would impose sanctions in response to the actions specified in the question.

QUESTIONS FOR THE RECORD SUBMITTED TO ROBERT EINHORN
HOUSE INTERNATIONAL RELATIONS COMMITTEE
MARCH 4, 1998

Questions from Representative Berman

Q.4. The certification materials indicate a rather high level of US confidence that China will not resume delivery of a uranium conversion facility, will not deliver any power reactors, and will not engage in any other nuclear cooperation with Iran beyond the two ongoing projects -- would the US regard any subsequent Sino-Iranian nuclear cooperation beyond these projects as a violation of the terms for resuming US nuclear cooperation with China?

A. Yes, with the possible exception of supply of medical isotopes or other similar use of nuclear materials in medicine or agriculture.

QUESTIONS FOR THE RECORD SUBMITTED TO ROBERT EINHORN
HOUSE INTERNATIONAL RELATIONS COMMITTEE
MARCH 4, 1998

Questions from Representative Berman

Q.5. Does China's pledge that it will not engage in any new nuclear cooperation with Iran extend to the delivery of nuclear dual-use goods? China has indicated that it will establish license requirements for dual-use goods on the Nuclear Suppliers Group trigger list -- has China ever given us any indication whatsoever that it will enforce a policy of denying applications for exports of nuclear dual-use goods destined for Iran?

A. We had extensive discussions with the Chinese about their safeguarded nuclear cooperation with Iran. China pledged that it would not engage in any new nuclear cooperation with Iran. We would regard a transfer of a nuclear-related dual-use good that could make a material contribution to Iran's nuclear program as a violation of that commitment.

QUESTIONS FOR THE RECORD SUBMITTED TO ROBERT EINHORN
HOUSE INTERNATIONAL RELATIONS COMMITTEE
MARCH 4, 1998

Questions from Representative Berman

Q.6. If the US resumes active nuclear cooperation with China while China continues to engage in nuclear cooperation with Iran, continues to deliver nuclear dual-use goods to Iran, and continues to engage in active nuclear cooperation with Pakistan without any requirement for full-scope safeguards, how will this cooperation affect US diplomatic efforts to discourage other countries from engaging in similar trade with both countries?

A. China has provided a clear assurance to the United States that it is not going to engage in new nuclear cooperation with Iran, and that it will complete its few existing projects--which are not of proliferation concern--within a relatively short period of time. We do not regard China's completion of these existing projects as having any adverse effect on US efforts to discourage other countries from assisting Iran's nuclear program. On the contrary, we think the fact that China will forgo all future nuclear cooperation with Iran beyond completion of those specified projects to be the point that will be significant to other governments.

As to the matter of Pakistan and full-scope safeguards, China has made a commitment not to provide assistance to unsafeguarded nuclear facilities, in Pakistan

50-151 98-8

or any other non-nuclear weapon state. China has not ruled out assistance to safeguarded nuclear facilities in Pakistan. However, all other major nuclear suppliers have made a commitment in the Nuclear Suppliers Group not to engage in significant nuclear cooperation with any non-nuclear weapon state (including Pakistan) in the absence of full-scope IAEA safeguards. We have no reason to think that any other supplier has reconsidered or would reconsider its commitment in this regard because of China's unwillingness thus far to join the consensus on requiring full-scope safeguards as a condition of export.

QUESTIONS FOR THE RECORD SUBMITTED TO ROBERT EINHORN
HOUSE INTERNATIONAL RELATIONS COMMITTEE
MARCH 4, 1998

Questions from Representative Berman

Q7. China will reportedly continue to assist Iran to build a facility to produce zirconium.

-- (a) Why does the Nuclear Suppliers Group include zirconium on its Trigger List?

A. The NSG and US control nuclear grade (hafnium free) zirconium because its neutron transparency and corrosion resistance make it the ideal material for nuclear fuel cladding and for reactor internals such as coolant channels.

-- (b) What is the licensing status of such a commodity under US export controls -- why does the US control exports of zirconium?

A. The US controls exports of nuclear grade zirconium tubing and zirconium components, such as fuel assembly hardware and reactor internals, under the US Atomic Energy Act. Such exports require a Nuclear Regulatory Commission license and are only approved for countries with the appropriate nonproliferation credentials which have provided written assurances to the United States confirming such conditions as the right of prior US consent for retransfers of supplied items. Such items are also subject to the NSG full-scope safeguards requirement.

Export of nuclear grade zirconium in unfabricated form is subject to the Department of Commerce nuclear nonproliferation controls. Such exports would not be approved in any case where there was a risk of nuclear explosive or unsafeguarded nuclear fuel cycle use.

-- (c) How about production facilities and related technology for zirconium, are these too controlled by both the Nuclear Suppliers Group and US nuclear export controls, and if so, why?

A. Complete fuel fabrication plants which would use zirconium tubing and hardware are controlled by the NSG and the US for nuclear nonproliferation reasons. However, zirconium production facilities and production technology are not controlled by either the NSG or the US.

-- (d) What significance do you attach to recent press reports that China has been seeking a zirconium plant from South Africa?

A. The Chinese purchased a plant from South Africa for the fabrication of zirconium nuclear fuel cladding tubes which the South Africans no longer need. Zirconium is the fuel cladding of choice for civilian nuclear power reactors and we attribute no significance to the fact that China is seeking to augment its domestic capability in this area.

-- (e) If, as the certification materials claim, the US regards any nuclear cooperation whatsoever with Iran as contributing to Iran's nuclear infrastructure and thereby its reported bomb program, then what is the justification for the continuation of the two remaining nuclear projects in Iran?

A. The only remaining cooperation between China and Iran involves training in the use of a small Chinese-supplied research reactor, which is subject to IAEA safeguards and inspection, and the development of a zirconium tube production facility - neither of which are proliferation sensitive. China has committed not to engage in any new nuclear cooperation with Iran and made clear that existing cooperation with Iran would be ended in a relatively short period of time.

-- (f) How will the US acquiescence to continued Chinese nuclear assistance to Iran in these two areas affect ongoing and future US efforts to discourage other countries from continuing their own peaceful nuclear assistance to Iran?

A. Since China has committed to end nuclear cooperation with Iran with the completion of the two projects described above, we see no detriment to our efforts to get other countries to cease nuclear cooperation with Iran. In fact, China's willingness to end nuclear cooperation with Iran will be helpful in our efforts with other suppliers.

-- (g) Has the US ever issued a diplomatic demarche to discourage any country from helping Iran to acquire zirconium or its production technology or equipment?

A. The United States encouraged China not to complete the transfer of zirconium fuel cladding production equipment and technology to Iran.

QUESTIONS FOR THE RECORD SUBMITTED TO ROBERT EINHORN
HOUSE INTERNATIONAL RELATIONS COMMITTEE
MARCH 4, 1998

Questions from Representative Berman

Q.9. China has historically engaged in far more dangerous nuclear cooperation with Pakistan than with Iran, yet the United States reportedly only insisted that China not commence new cooperation with Iran -- why did the US not insist upon a halt to all Chinese nuclear cooperation with Pakistan, given this unfortunate track record?

A. Iran and Pakistan present different situations, and US policy on China's nuclear cooperation with the two countries has to be tailored to the circumstances of each.

During our discussions with China we have stated our position that China should not cooperate with Iran on nuclear matters because we believe this cooperation could assist Iran in its nuclear weapons program.

When discussing cooperation with Pakistan, we have pointed out to the Chinese the difficulties of cooperation with a country that has both safeguarded and unsafeguarded programs. The Chinese have taken note of our concerns, but at this point they are not prepared to accept the NSG policy of requiring full-scope safeguards as a condition of export. Such acceptance is not required by the NPT, nor does US law or policy require it as a condition for implementing agreements for cooperation. It is too early to tell how

Pakistan's recent nuclear explosive tests will affect China's policy in this area.

QUESTIONS FOR THE RECORD SUBMITTED TO ROBERT EINHORN
HOUSE INTERNATIONAL RELATIONS COMMITTEE
MARCH 4, 1998

Questions from Representative Berman

Q.11. Will the US permit cooperation to continue if China:

(a) Licenses and ships nuclear dual-use goods to Pakistan's safeguarded nuclear program?

A. Yes. We expect that China will continue to support Pakistan's safeguarded nuclear program, although we do not yet know how Pakistan's nuclear explosive tests will affect Chinese policy in this area.

(b) Licenses and delivers nuclear dual-use goods to unsafeguarded facilities in Pakistan?

A. Exports of listed dual-use items to an unsafeguarded facility would be inconsistent with China's commitments not to provide assistance to unsafeguarded facilities in Pakistan or anywhere else.

(c) Assists Pakistan in the safeguarded production of enriched uranium or the separation of plutonium?

(d) Assists Pakistan in the construction of a plutonium production reactor under safeguards?

A. While China has not made a commitment to avoid cooperation with safeguarded uranium enrichment or plutonium production facilities in Pakistan, this is an entirely hypothetical issue. Pakistan has strongly refused to place safeguards on its uranium enrichment and plutonium production programs.

(e) Engages in future technical discussions or exchanges of personnel from nuclear weapons facilities in both countries?

A. No, with the presumption that such discussions or exchanges involve cooperation in the acquisition of nuclear weapons. As just noted, our cooperation with China is premised in part on China's commitment to avoid assistance to unsafeguarded facilities in Pakistan. From Chinese official directives and statements, we are confident that China shares our understanding that "assistance" covers transfers of technology and information (not just hardware and material), and that China's pledge precludes assistance both to unsafeguarded nuclear fuel cycle facilities and nuclear explosives programs in all non-nuclear weapon states including Pakistan.

(f) Fails to take steps that are adequate to ensure against the diversion of Chinese nuclear items either from safeguarded to unsafeguarded programs in Pakistan, or via reexports from third countries?

A. We would take a careful look at all relevant factors, and assess the degree of possible Chinese Government responsibility either active or passive as compared with the responsibility of the entity actually carrying out the diversion, as well as China's willingness to cease cooperation with a country where a diversion had occurred.

QUESTIONS FOR THE RECORD SUBMITTED TO ROBERT EINHORN
HOUSE INTERNATIONAL RELATIONS COMMITTEE
MARCH 4, 1998

Questions from Representative Berman

Q.12 With respect to China's "catch-all" export licensing clause -- Does the regulation require licensing officials to deny licenses for the export of goods which an exporter knows or has reason to know will be used for a nuclear weapons-related purpose, whether or not the specific good or technology is on any control list?

A. This authority is included in what China calls their "case-by-case" authority. If the relevant Chinese government department has reason to believe that the export of some item may possibly cause nuclear proliferation, even though the item may not be listed, the department concerned has the right to ban or suspend such an export.

QUESTIONS FOR THE RECORD SUBMITTED TO ROBERT EINHORN
HOUSE INTERNATIONAL RELATIONS COMMITTEE
MARCH 4, 1998

Rep. Berman Questions

Q.13 The DIA includes China's key nuclear groups--The China National Nuclear Corporation and The China Nuclear Energy Industry Corporation--in an unclassified wall chart of China's "Defense-Industrial Trading Organizations" -- how are these entities tied to China's defense establishment?

A. The answer to this question is provided by INR and is included in the classified responses.

-- If US/China nuclear trade resumes, would these be the entities with which US nuclear companies would likely cooperate? What were the respective role of these enterprises in the ring magnet affair?

A. If US/China nuclear trade resumes, we anticipate that the majority of cooperation would be between US companies and CNNC, including its subsidiary the Chinese Nuclear Energy Industry Corporation (CNEIC). CNEIC and the China Zhongyuan Engineering Corporation (CZEC) -- also a subsidiary of CNNC -- are the only two companies authorized by the Chinese government to conduct exports of nuclear (i.e. not dual-use) items. In March, the Chinese government announced a major reorganization of CNNC. It is not clear what impact this reorganization will have on the relationship of CNEIC and CZEC to CNNC.

During an investigation of the ring magnet affair, the Secretary of State concluded that the transfer had occurred but that there was not a sufficient basis to conclude that the government of China had acted willfully. Although CNEIC, the entity responsible for the transfer of the ring magnets, is a government-owned entity, we do not know how individual transactions were notified and approved between the CNEIC and other Chinese entities. Many Chinese entities, even government-owned ones, operate with considerable autonomy. Moreover, senior Chinese government officials have denied authoritatively that central Chinese government officials knew of the ring magnet transfer and we have no information that would contradict that assertion.

QUESTIONS FOR THE RECORD SUBMITTED TO ROBERT EINHORN
HOUSE INTERNATIONAL RELATIONS COMMITTEE
MARCH 4, 1998

Questions from Representative Berman

Q.14. Do we have clear and unequivocal assurances that China is not assisting and will not assist any non-nuclear weapon state, either directly or indirectly, in acquiring nuclear explosive devices or the material and components for such devices?

-- Do we believe those assurances?

A. By virtue of its March 1992 adherence to the Treaty on the Nonproliferation of Nuclear Weapons (NPT), China has undertaken not to transfer to any recipient whatsoever nuclear weapons or other nuclear explosive devices or control over such weapons or explosive devices directly, or indirectly; and not in any way to assist, encourage, or induce any non-nuclear weapons state to manufacture or otherwise assist a nonnuclear weapon state to acquire nuclear weapons or other nuclear explosive devices, or control over such weapons or explosive devices. Article III.2 of the NPT also requires the parties to the Treaty not to provide: a) source or special fissionable material, or b) equipment or material especially designed or prepared for the processing, use or production of special fissionable material, to any non-nuclear-weapon state for peaceful purposes, unless the source or special fissionable material shall be subject to the safeguards of the International Atomic Energy Agency (IAEA).

In addition, China issued a statement in May 1996 that it will not provide assistance to unsafeguarded nuclear facilities, and has made clear that this prohibition also applies to assistance to nuclear explosive activities. China also joined the Zangger Committee which has established guidelines for the implementation of Article III.2 of the NPT.

As noted in the answers to other questions, China has established nuclear export controls on nuclear materials, equipment and technology as well as nuclear-related dual-use items in order to implement these assurances. These controls also apply to exchange of personnel and technological data.

China appears to be living up to its commitments and assurances.

QUESTIONS FOR THE RECORD SUBMITTED TO ROBERT EINHORN
HOUSE INTERNATIONAL RELATIONS COMMITTEE
MARCH 4, 1998

Questions from Representative Berman

Q.15 Did the May 1996 commitment not to provide assistance to unsafeguarded facilities include technical assistance in our view?

A. Yes. On many occasions we discussed with Chinese officials our definition of assistance as including more than equipment and materials, and extending to technical assistance including exchanges of personnel. Based on these discussions, there is a substantial degree of understanding between us on what it means to assist an unsafeguarded facility.

QUESTIONS FOR THE RECORD SUBMITTED TO ROBERT EINHORN
HOUSE INTERNATIONAL RELATIONS COMMITTEE
MARCH 4, 1998

Questions from Representative Berman

Q.16 Have we verified that the June 1997 list of controlled nuclear items the Chinese have stated is identical to the Nuclear Suppliers Group trigger list but do we know that it is identical? (sic)

A. We have reviewed the June 1997 control list provided by China. We believe that it is substantively identical to the Nuclear Suppliers Group trigger list. We would also note that China has since become a member of the NPT Exporters (Zangger) Committee, and is thereby obligated to control essentially the same trigger list.

-- Could you provide us with a copy of that list?

A. We have not yet transcribed the Chinese list into English item by item. We will be happy to provide an English translation of the Chinese-language control list when it is completed.

QUESTIONS FOR THE RECORD SUBMITTED TO ROBERT EINHORN
HOUSE INTERNATIONAL RELATIONS COMMITTEE
MARCH 4, 1998

Questions from Representative Berman

Q.17 The September 1997 list of controlled nuclear items the Chinese state is identical to the NSG trigger list but do we know it is identical?

A. We have translated the September 1997 control list provided by China. Based on an analysis of the translation we believe that it is substantively identical to the nuclear trigger list adopted by the Nuclear Suppliers Group.

-- Could you provide us with that list?

A. The Chinese requested that we treat this list confidentially. We would be happy to show you the list upon request, or to provide it as a classified document.

QUESTIONS FOR THE RECORD SUBMITTED TO ROBERT EINHORN
HOUSE INTERNATIONAL RELATIONS COMMITTEE
MARCH 4, 1998

Questions from Representative Berman

Q.18 The Chinese stated in October 1997 that its regulations strictly prohibit any exchange of nuclear weapons-related technology with other countries and provide for a denial of assistance to nuclear explosive activities.

- Have we seen a copy of those regulations?

A. Yes. In May 1997 the Chinese issued a State Council Decree titled "State Council Notice Regarding Strict Implementation of China's Nuclear Export Policy."

- Could you provide us with a copy?

A. Yes. An English translation is attached.

UNOFFICIAL TRANSLATION

**STATE COUNCIL NOTICE
REGARDING STRICT IMPLEMENTATION OF
CHINA'S NUCLEAR EXPORT POLICY**

To all Provinces, Autonomous Regions, Directly-Administered Municipal People's Governments, and all ministries, commissions and other agencies directly under the State Council:

China advocates a comprehensive ban and thorough destruction of nuclear weapons and other weapons of mass destruction. China carries out a policy of "not advocating, not encouraging, and not carrying out nuclear weapons proliferation, and not assisting other countries in developing nuclear weapons." China, as an NPT Contracting Party, has always adopted a solemn and responsible attitude in the area of nuclear export controls.

In order to ensure that China's nuclear trade is carried out in accordance with relevant national regulations, and consistent with international norms and methods, all relevant departments and work units must faithfully implement China's nuclear export policy in carrying out foreign economic and trade activities. The nuclear export policy is: to not advocate, encourage, or carry out nuclear weapons proliferation and not assist other countries in developing nuclear weapons; nuclear export items are to be used only for peaceful purposes, under IAEA safeguards, and not allowing their transfer to a third party without China's permission; and to not provide assistance to any nuclear facility which does not accept IAEA safeguards. Following are the relevant notifications:

1. The export of nuclear materials, nuclear facilities, nuclear technology, and non-nuclear materials used in reactors will be exclusively undertaken by China National Nuclear Corporation and other Government-designated corporations. All other departments or corporations are not permitted to engage in this trade.

2. Nuclear materials, nuclear facilities and relevant technologies, non-nuclear materials used in reactors, and nuclear-related dual-use equipment, materials, and related technologies (specific lists will be published by the MFA, MOFTEC and the China Atomic Energy Authority) exported by China may not be provided to or used in nuclear facilities which do not accept IAEA safeguards. All departments and

corporations are not permitted to cooperate with any nuclear facility which does not accept IAEA safeguards, and are not permitted to engage in the exchange of technical personnel or technical information.

3. Some nuclear facilities of non-participants of the NPT accept IAEA safeguards and some do not (a list of NPT Contracting Parties will be provided separately). Because of this, in cooperating with a non-NPT country in export trade or cooperative activities listed in paragraph 2, if these activities involve the other side's nuclear facilities, Chinese entities shall first verify with the China Atomic Energy Authority (China National Nuclear Corporation) whether this facility is under IAEA safeguards, and moreover should ask the relevant department of the importing country government to provide an end-use certificate and guarantee that the imported items or planned cooperation will not be diverted to a nuclear facility not under IAEA safeguards. If cooperation does not involve a nuclear facility on the other side, the Chinese entity should ask the relevant department of the importing government to provide certification in advance, provide a reasonable and credible end-user certificate for the imported items, and guarantee that the imported items or the planned cooperation between the two sides in these items will not be diverted to a nuclear facility not under safeguards. These certifications must be confirmed and approved by the Foreign Ministry, MOFTEC, and the China Atomic Energy Authority before an export or cooperative activity may take place.

State Council of the People's Republic of China
(seal)

May 27, 1997

QUESTIONS FOR THE RECORD SUBMITTED TO ROBERT EINHORN
HOUSE INTERNATIONAL RELATIONS COMMITTEE
MARCH 4, 1998

Questions from Representative Berman

Q.19 Could you describe the nuclear export control system reportedly established by the Chinese on May 27, 1997, and how it works?

A. In May 1997 the State Council issued a Notice "Regarding Strict Implementation of China's Nuclear Export Policy." This notice was sent to all governmental and nongovernmental entities involved in nuclear and nuclear-related dual-use exports.

The Notice reiterates China's nuclear policy "to not advocate, encourage, or carry out nuclear weapons proliferation and not assist other countries in developing nuclear weapons; nuclear export items are to be used only for peaceful purposes, under IAEA safeguards, and not allowing their transfer to a third party without China's permission; and not to provide assistance to any nuclear facility which does not accept IAEA safeguards".

The Notice restricts the export of nuclear materials, facilities, technology, and non-nuclear materials used in reactors to the China National Nuclear Corporation (CNNC). The Notice states that nuclear materials, facilities and relevant technologies, non-nuclear materials used in reactors, and nuclear-related dual-use equipment, materials and related technology -- including the exchange of technical personnel or technical information -- may not be provided to or used in nuclear facilities which do not accept IAEA safeguards.

Exporters are required to verify with the China Atomic Energy Authority (CAEA) the safeguards status of a recipient facility. They are also required to obtain an end-use certificate from the importing country, and guarantees that the items or planned cooperation will not be diverted to an unsafeguarded nuclear facility. When cooperation does not involve a nuclear facility, the exporter is required to obtain from the importing government an end-user certificate and guarantee that the item or cooperation will not be diverted to an unsafeguarded facility. All end-user certificates and non-diversion guarantees must be confirmed and approved by the Foreign Ministry, MOFTEC, and the CAEA before cooperation may begin.

The May Directive was supplemented by a control list substantively identical to the Nuclear Suppliers Group dual-use list.

QUESTIONS FOR THE RECORD SUBMITTED TO ROBERT EINHORN
HOUSE INTERNATIONAL RELATIONS COMMITTEE
MARCH 4, 1998

Questions from Representative Berman

Q.20. How many times and when have senior Chinese officials assured us that they were abiding by their nonproliferation commitments?

A. Chinese officials have made many assurances over the years. The key question is whether Chinese behavior has been consistent with Chinese assurances.

In the 1990s, and especially since May 1996, we have seen a marked, positive shift in China's nuclear nonproliferation behavior. China has taken important steps that demonstrate its growing acceptance of nuclear nonproliferation norms -- examples include adherence to the NPT and support for its indefinite and unconditional extension, termination of nuclear testing and signature of the CTBT, support for a Fissile Material Cutoff Treaty, and support for the strengthened safeguards system of the IAEA.

China's cooperation with the US on cases of concern and establishment of a nationwide nuclear export control system over the past two years are important practical steps which give further substance to their commitments. Chinese officials appear to be acting at a qualitatively different level of seriousness and commitment now than in the past.

Taken together, these various steps and developments constitute a marked, positive shift in China's nuclear nonproliferation policies and practices.

QUESTIONS FOR THE RECORD SUBMITTED TO ROBERT EINHORN
HOUSE INTERNATIONAL RELATIONS COMMITTEE
MARCH 4, 1998

Questions from Representative Berman

Q.21. Have the Chinese provided the Director General of the IAEA full and complete information on its exports and imports of nuclear material since its November 1991 commitment to do so?

A. On November 29, 1991, China sent a letter to the Director General of the International Atomic Energy Agency (IAEA) informing him that, in the interest of assisting the Agency in its safeguards activities, China has decided to provide the IAEA with information on exports and imports of nuclear material.

The Chinese letter is contained in the Agency publication INFCIRC 207. Reporting under INFCIRC 207 is "safeguards confidential." However, we have no reason to believe that China is not providing information of exports and imports of nuclear material in accordance with its letter of November 29, 1991 to the IAEA Director General.

QUESTIONS FOR THE RECORD SUBMITTED TO ROBERT EINHORN
HOUSE INTERNATIONAL RELATIONS COMMITTEE
MARCH 4, 1998

Questions from Representative Berman

Q.22. Does the US have the right to confirm through on-site visits the use of all items subject to the nuclear cooperation Agreement?

-- What assurances do we have that the Chinese will permit such visits take place in a timely fashion--such as not been the case in regard to our MOU concerning customs inspections of Chinese prison labor products?

A. Article 8 of the US-China Peaceful Nuclear Cooperation Agreement provides for the establishment of mutually acceptable arrangements for exchanges of information and visits to material, facilities and components subject to the Agreement. We have concluded a memorandum of understanding which contains obligations specifying the types of information exchanges and the content, occasion and frequency of visits. Since cooperation under the Agreement is contingent on the fulfillment of the obligations relating to exchanges of information and visits we have every reason to believe that China will abide by the obligations it has assumed in the memorandum of understanding.

Question for the Record Submitted to Robert Einhorn
House International Relations Committee
March 4, 1998

Question:

In attempting to monitor the end use of sensitive items in China, the Commerce Department has regularly encountered minimal cooperation and support from the Chinese government.

- In light of this background of few if any Post Shipment Verifications undertaken in China and in light of the fact that it only issued new export control regulations in September of 1997 at American insistence, what indications are there that they are being fully implemented and enforced?

- Would it not be more prudent for U.S. policy makers to ensure that China has put these regulations into practice - and has provided for penalties for violations and has shown that it is willing to levy these penalties on those entities that have violated the regulations - before approving a wide range of nuclear-related licenses for China?

Answer:

The Commerce Department provides the following answer: The Commerce Department has been working through the U.S.-China Joint Commission on Commerce and Trade (JCCT) to make progress with China on end-use checks, including post shipment verifications. Secretary Daley discussed end-use checks with his counterpart Minister Wu Yi in October 1997.

As a follow-up to the JCCT initiative, a Chinese delegation is scheduled to come to Washington on April 6 for an export controls seminar. This seminar will present an opportunity to learn more about China's export controls and enforcement.

Because the nuclear agreement has not yet been fully implemented, the Commerce Department has not approved any licenses for nuclear-related commodities to nuclear end-users in China.

Question for the Record Submitted to Robert Einhorn
House International Relations Committee
March 4, 1998

Question:

The Administration has yet to demonstrate to Congress that it has put in place procedures and mechanisms designed to address the criticisms of the General Accounting Office in its 1994 study of licensing procedures for dual-use nuclear exports. In its study, the GAO found inadequate criteria for selecting pre-license checks and post-shipment verifications, ineffective methods used to perform these inspections and lack of verification of government to government assurances against nuclear end uses.

- Why does China still insist that no post-shipment verifications (PSV's) can be undertaken by U.S. Government officials to check on the end use of our dual use exports to China?

Answer:

The Department of Commerce believes your premise is incorrect and provides the following response to the premise. The Department of Commerce has put in place procedures and mechanisms designed to address the criticisms of the GAO. The Bureau of Export Administration (BXA) has identified those controlled nuclear-related commodities which should have the greatest priority for the conduct of pre-license checks and post-shipment verification and has forwarded this information to all pertinent employees for their use in reviewing export license transactions and selecting PLC and PSV candidates. This information is used in selecting candidates for on-site PLC and PSV visits by Export Enforcement personnel. BXA's Safeguards Teams conduct very detailed on-site PLCs and PSVs, confirming that the commodities will be or are being used in accordance with license conditions.

In addition, BXA provided detailed instructions to its special agents and FCS officers stationed abroad concerning the procedures for conducting nuclear-related PLCs and PSVs.

With respect to your question about post shipment verifications in China, China sees these checks as an attack on its sovereignty. BXA is working with officials of China's Ministry of Foreign Trade and Economic Cooperation (MOFTEC) on end-use checks. Commerce Under Secretary William Reinsch will be addressing this issue on March 25-27 while he is Beijing.

○